Reflections

Thirty **MORE** sparkling gems

Peter Currie

DayOne

© Day One Publications 2022
First Edition 2022

Unless otherwise indicated, Scripture quotations are from the New King
James Version (NKJV)®. Copyright © 1982 by Thomas Nelson, Inc.
Used by permission. All rights reserved.

British Library Cataloguing in Publication Data available

ISBN 978-1-84625-722-3

Published by Day One Publications
Ryelands Road, Leominster, HR6 8NZ

☎ 01568 613 740
FAX: 01568 611 473
email—sales@dayone.co.uk
web site—www.dayone.co.uk

Cover designed by Kathryn Chedgzoy and printed by 4Edge

This book is dedicated to the many humble
Christians I have known over the years,
whose sterling faith and Christlike lives have
exemplified the reality of the promises of God.

Endorsement

In a world of promise making and promise breaking, when a person's word is no longer their bond, when it is hard to discern what is truth, we need to listen well to the promises of God. It is essential for every Christian to think carefully about them, and allow the truth to penetrate their heart and transform their life.

Once again, Peter Currie has gathered thirty more promises found throughout the Old and New Testaments that are surely worth pondering in our rather hurried and busy lives. I am grateful to Peter not only for selecting these out and sharing his thoughts, but also for displaying in his life a concrete trust and joy in these precious promises for all to see.

These promises are given for all who are trusting in the Saviour, to help them live lives worthy of the Lord Jesus Christ, as they wait, 'looking for the blessed hope and glorious appearing of our great God and Saviour Jesus Christ' (Titus 2:13).

Each of the promises will do your heart good and be kept by the God whose word is unwavering.

Stuart Davis
Co-Pastor at Trinity Road Chapel, London

Contents

Introduction

The promises of God recorded in the Bible are not only numerous. Each one is important in its own right and of great worth—'exceedingly great and precious', as the apostle Peter puts it (2 Peter 1:4). The Bible is like a treasure chest and each promise is like a sparkling gem contained therein. This book is a sequel to my book *Thirty Sparkling Gems*. It contains, as the title implies, meditations on thirty more of the precious promises of God, which I hope will provide much help, strength, assurance and joy to God's children and perhaps even lead some to put their trust in the Lord Jesus Christ as their Saviour for the first time.

The selection I have chosen starts with six of the compound names of Deity from the Old Testament which tell us what God promises to be to His people. Then there are six promises given by our Lord Jesus Christ Himself while here on earth, followed by six promises from the book of Psalms. Finally, there are four promises for the Christian life, five promises of a reward in heaven and three promises of a glorious future for all who are genuinely trusting in the Lord Jesus Christ as their Saviour.

Part 1: What God promises to be to his people

Moses was tending a flock of sheep near Mount Sinai when God spoke to him from the midst of the burning bush and said, 'I will send you to Pharaoh that you may bring my people, the children of Israel, out of Egypt' (Exodus 3:10). In reply, Moses asked a number of questions. One of these questions concerned the name of God:

> Then Moses said to God, 'Indeed, when I come to the children of Israel and say to them, "The God of your fathers has sent me to you," and they say to me, "What is His name?" what shall I say to them?' And God said to Moses, 'I AM WHO I AM.' And He said, 'Thus you shall say to the children of Israel, "I AM has sent me to you."' Moreover, God said to Moses, 'Thus you shall say to the children of Israel: "The LORD God of your fathers, the God of Abraham, the God of Isaac, and the God of Jacob, has sent me to you. This is My name forever, and this is My memorial to all generations"' (Exod. 3:13–15).

The Hebrew word translated 'LORD' is transliterated as 'Jehovah' or 'Yahweh'. There is some uncertainty which is right because the Hebrew alphabet does not have any vowels as such. It does have *vowel points* (marks inserted to indicate a vowel), but these are omitted for this word, which was considered the most sacred name for the Almighty (Jewish people say the word 'Adonay' instead when reading the Hebrew in public—this is the word translated 'Lord' in the NKJV of Genesis 15:2). Also, some say that two of the Hebrew consonant letters should be pronounced 'J' and 'v', whereas others say they should be pronounced 'Y' and 'w'. Either way, the meaning of 'Jehovah' (my preference) is 'The One who is',[1] and it is easy to see how this connects with God saying to Moses that His name is 'I AM'.

The meditations that follow consider the six compound names based on 'Jehovah' which we find in the Old Testament. These names show us what God promises to be to His people. For example, the first is *Jehovah-Jireh* which means 'The-LORD-Will-Provide'. God promises to be the Provider of His people. This includes material provision, but it means far more than that as we shall see. These compound names are indeed very rich in meaning and I trust that the meditations on them will be of much blessing to my readers.

The~LORD~ Will~Provide (Jehovah~Jireh)

And Abraham called the name of the place, The-LORD-Will-Provide; as it is said to this day, 'In the Mount of the LORD it shall be provided.'

(Gen. 22:14)

O ur text refers to a mountain in the land of Moriah. The KJV gives the name of the place as 'Jehovah-Jireh'. This is a transliteration of the Hebrew (both Hebrew and Greek have different alphabets to English). The NKJV gives the meaning of 'Jehovah-Jireh' as 'The-LORD-Will-Provide'. This reminds us that God is the One who provides for us materially, who supplies 'all ... [our] need according to His riches in glory by Christ Jesus' (Phil. 4:19). This is true, but when we look at the context, we realize that there is much more to it than that.

Genesis chapter 22 begins with the command to sacrifice Isaac 'as a burnt offering on one of the mountains of which I shall tell you' (Gen. 22:2). This was a very great test of Abraham's faith. The first time the word 'provide' appears is in verse 8. In reply to Isaac's question 'Where is the lamb for a burnt offering?' (Gen. 22:7), Abraham says, 'God will provide for Himself the lamb for a burnt offering' (Gen. 22:8).

When Abraham 'took the knife to slay his son' (Gen. 22:10), he was told to stop and God provided 'a ram caught in a thicket by its horns' to act as a substitute for Isaac (Gen. 22:13). However, that is not all. Our text speaks about the future—it says 'The-LORD-Will-Provide', not 'The-LORD-Has-Provided'. As a matter of fact, the KJV of Genesis 22:8 omits the word 'for' and says that 'God will provide *Himself* a lamb for a burnt offering,' and this was literally fulfilled when the Lord Jesus Christ went to Calvary's Cross as 'The Lamb of God who takes away the sin of the world' (John 1:29).

I believe Abraham foresaw Calvary's Cross. The Lord Jesus Christ definitely said that 'Abraham rejoiced to see My day, and he saw it' (John 8:56), and so when Abraham said 'God will provide for Himself the lamb for a burnt-offering' (Gen. 22:8), and when he saw the ram caught in a thicket and called the name of the place Jehovah-Jireh, I believe that he was being enabled to look ahead to Calvary's Cross. Of course, he saw it afar off in type and shadow, but he did see it (see Heb. 11:13).

Martin Luther once read this story for family devotions. When he had finished, his wife said, 'I do not believe it. God would not have treated his son [meaning Isaac] like that.' 'But, Katie,' answered Luther, 'He did' [meaning how He treated the Lord Jesus Christ].[1] As John 3:16 says, 'God so loved the world that He gave His only begotten Son,'—because there was no other way by which sinful people like you and me could be saved.

The place where Abraham was commanded to sacrifice Isaac was a mountain in the land of Moriah. It could well have been the very mountain on which Solomon's temple was built many years later (see 2 Chr. 3:1), and it was probably not far from 'the place called Calvary' where our Lord Jesus Christ was crucified (Luke 23:33). Thus was the saying, 'In the Mount of the LORD it shall be provided' (Gen. 22:14), fulfilled. Just as

Abraham was commanded to sacrifice his son Isaac whom he loved, even so God the Father really did sacrifice His beloved Son, His darling Son, the Lord Jesus Christ, so that 'whoever … [trusts] in Him should not perish but have everlasting life' (John 3:16).

> To God be the glory, great things He hath done!
> So loved He the world that He gave us His Son;
> Who yielded His life an atonement for sin,
> And opened the life-gate that all may go in.
>
> O perfect redemption, the purchase of blood,
> To every believer the promise of God;
> The vilest offender who truly believes,
> That moment from Jesus a pardon receives.
>
> *Praise the Lord! praise the Lord!*
> *Let the earth hear His voice!*
> *Praise the Lord! praise the Lord!*
> *Let the people rejoice!*
> *Oh, come to the Father, through Jesus the Son:*
> *And give Him the glory; great things He hath done!*
> (Fanny Crosby, 1820–1915)

The Lord Who Heals You (Jehovah~Rapha)

If you diligently heed the voice of the LORD your God and do what is right in His sight, give ear to His commandments and keep all His statutes, I will put none of the diseases on you which I have brought on the Egyptians. For I am the LORD who heals you.

(Exod. 15:26).

Jehovah-Rapha is the second of the six 'Jehovah' compound names which we are considering. The NKJV translates it as, 'the LORD who heals you'. The Hebrew word for *healing* is an interesting one. Literally, it means, 'to mend by stitching'.[1] It can refer to physical healing and also to things being restored to what they ought to be. For example, Jeremiah 19:11 uses this word and speaks about 'a potter's vessel, which cannot be made whole again'.

When the Lord Jesus Christ was on earth, He was 'the LORD who heals you'. The Bible says that He 'healed all who were sick' (Matt. 8:16). However, the greatest act of 'healing' was when He went to Calvary's Cross so that all who trust in Him can be completely cured of the deadly disease of sin and restored to friendship with God (see Isa. 53:5).

All the bitter experiences of life can be 'healed' as well. The context of the promise we are considering is the bitter waters of Marah. First the Israelites had no water, then bitter water (see Exod. 15:22–23). So, what did they do? The Bible says they 'complained against Moses' (Exod. 15:24). Life made them bitter. It turned them against God's servant Moses who had led them out of Egypt. However, it did not make Moses bitter.

The Bible says, 'he cried out to the LORD,' and God heard and answered his prayer. God 'healed' the bitter waters by means of 'a tree' (Exod. 15:25).

In the New Testament, the Cross of the Lord Jesus Christ is referred to as *a tree*. Writing to Christians, the apostle Peter says that the Lord 'bore our sins in His own body on the tree' (1 Peter 2:24). Upon the Cross, He bore our sins in such a way that He was treated as though He were the sinner and punished instead, 'the just for the unjust' (1 Peter. 3:18).

When life threatens to make us bitter, Christians can remember that the Lord Jesus bore their sins upon the Cross. Sins forgiven and life everlasting are the portion of whoever believes and trusts in Him (see Acts 10:43; John 3:16). What a cheerful message this is! How well-suited to heal the bitter experiences of life!

A day is coming when all sickness will be healed, all sin will be banished and all bitterness will be forgotten. God will 'make all things new' (Rev. 21:5), and all things will be restored to how they ought to be. The whole universe will be mended. The Bible promises that those who genuinely trust in the Lord Jesus Christ as their Saviour (the overcomers) 'shall inherit all things,' but those who go with the flow, refuse to trust in the Saviour and refuse to repent of their sins will not (see Rev. 21:7–8). The promise of healing in our text was for the Israelites not the Egyptians. Likewise, the wonderful things that God has prepared are for those who belong to His people, not for an unbelieving world. Reader, to which do you belong?

O the bitter shame and sorrow,
That a time could ever be,
When I let the Saviour's pity
Plead in vain and proudly answered,
'All of self and none of Thee!'

Yet He found me, I beheld Him
Bleeding on the accursed tree,
Heard Him pray, 'Forgive them, Father!'
And my wistful heart said faintly,
'Some of self and some of Thee!'

Day by day His tender mercy,
Healing, helping, full and free,
Sweet and strong and ah! so patient,
Brought me lower, while I whispered,
'Less of self and more of Thee!'

Higher than the highest heavens,
Deeper than the deepest sea,
Lord, Thy love at last has conquered;
Grant me now my supplication—
'None of self and all of Thee!'
(Theodore Monod , 1836–1921)

The~Lord~Is~ My~Banner (Jehovah~Nissi)

And Moses built an altar and called its name, The-Lord-Is-My-Banner; for he said, 'Because the Lord has sworn: the Lord will have war with Amalek from generation to generation.'

(Exod. 17:15–16)

The altar in our text commemorated a great victory. The Israelites had been saved from Egypt, but they found that they still had battles to fight. The Egyptians were not the only enemy. The Bible says that 'Amalek came and fought with Israel in Rephidim' (Exod. 17:8).

The Amalekites were a war-like tribe who were originally descended from Esau, Israel's twin brother (Amalek was one of Esau's grandsons—see Gen. 36:12). Joshua had to choose some men and fight with the Amalekites (see Exod. 17:9–10a), but he could not prevail without God's help. 'When Moses held up his hand ... Israel prevailed; and when he let down his hand, Amalek prevailed,' (see 17:10b–13)—the holding up of Moses' hand with the rod of God in it symbolized the invocation of divine aid.

Christians also have to fight—not against people, but against the world of sin, the flesh, and the devil. I think we can compare Egypt to the world of sin and Pharaoh to the devil, but we have another enemy as well. The Bible says, 'For the flesh lusts against the Spirit, and the Spirit against the flesh; and these are contrary to one another, so that you do not do the things that you wish' (Gal. 5:17). In this verse 'the flesh' means the sinful nature that still dwells within us, even though we are Christians. Just as Israel had to fight against their own relatives, those close to them according to the flesh, even so two natures exist within every born-again believer—the old and the new—and this is why we are conscious of a struggle within.

If we say we have no sinful nature, 'we deceive ourselves', says the apostle John (1 John 1:8). Christians want to stop doing evil and start doing good, but there is an enemy within. Victory is possible, but so is defeat. Just as Joshua could not prevail without God's help, so it is with us. This is why God has sent forth the Holy Spirit into our hearts (Gal. 4:6). If our behaviour is governed and guided by the Spirit, we shall be victorious and bring forth a wonderful harvest of Christian character, because it is God the Holy Spirit who is fighting for us (see Gal. 5:16–18, 22–23).

This is the meaning of the banner in our text. A banner shows for whom you are fighting and who is fighting for you. We are on the Lord's side and His resources are available to us. Every Christian can say, 'The-LORD-Is-My-Banner'. Only let us be careful to ensure that our behaviour is governed and guided by the Word of God. Otherwise, the Holy Spirit will be grieved and His power in our lives will be quenched (see Eph. 4:30; 1 Thes. 5:19). The Word and the Spirit go together—they are two sides of the same coin.

Christians are often conscious of a struggle. Our text says that the war with Amalek would be ongoing. The goal is not attained in this life. We should always be pressing on, not resting on our laurels but seeking to make progress by daily confessing and forsaking our sins, *looking to God for the help that we need* (see Phil. 3:12–14; 1 John 1:8–9; Prov. 28:13).

> Ho, my comrades! see the signal
> Waving in the sky!
> Reinforcements now appearing,
> Victory is nigh!
>
> See the mighty host advancing,
> Satan leading on:
> Mighty men around us falling,
> Courage almost gone!
>
> See the glorious banner waving!
> Hear the trumpet blow!
> In our Leader's name we'll triumph
> Over every foe!
>
> *'Hold the fort, for I am coming!'*
> *Jesus signals still;*
> *Wave the answer back to heaven,*
> *'By Thy grace we will!'*
> (P.P. Bliss, 1838–76)

The~LORD~ Is~Peace (Jehovah~Shalom)

So, Gideon built an altar there to the LORD, and called it
The-LORD-Is-Peace.

(Judg. 6:24a)

The Israelites were in trouble! Judges chapter 6 tells us that they 'did evil in the sight of the LORD. So the LORD delivered them into the hand of Midian for seven years' (Judg. 6:1). But then 'the Angel of the LORD' appeared to Gideon (see Judg. 6:11–12; this was a pre-incarnate appearance of the Lord Jesus Christ in human form). To start with, Gideon thought he was speaking to a fellow human being, but soon he began to realize that he was speaking to God. He made sure this was the case, and then he was afraid because he knew he had 'seen the Angel of the LORD face to face' (Judg. 6:22).

Anyone who has a conviction of sin feels unfit to stand before God in their own merits, knowing they deserve to die (e.g. Isa. 6:5). However, 'the LORD said to [Gideon], "Peace be with you; do not fear, you shall not die"' (Judg. 6:23), and so we come to our text. God had spoken the word of peace to Gideon, but Gideon knew there had to be shedding of blood. This is why he 'built an altar' (the Hebrew word translated 'altar' means 'a place of slaughter', according to *The New Compact Bible Dictionary*).[1] 'Without shedding of blood there is no remission' (Heb. 9:22), and no peace.

All this looks forward to the Lord Jesus Christ and the shedding of His precious blood. The Bible says that 'He Himself is our peace' (Eph. 2:14a), but not without the shedding of blood. Christians have been 'brought near by the blood of Christ' (Eph. 2:13). Peace has been made 'through the blood of His cross' (Col. 1:20b). 'The-Lord-is-Peace' is fulfilled in the Lord Jesus Christ. He is *Jehovah-Shalom*, who has given us 'peace with God' by the shedding of His blood (Rom. 5:1).

Peace with God means friendship with God, an unchanging relationship, but there is also 'the peace of God', an inward experience which 'surpasses all understanding'. It protects our hearts and minds from the harmful effects of anxiety, and it does this 'through Christ Jesus'—in virtue of who He is and what He has done for us (see Phil. 4:6–7). I will say more about this in a later meditation.

After God had spoken the word of peace to Gideon, he was sent out to do the work that God wanted him to do—he had already been told to 'go ... you shall save Israel' in Judges 6:14. The same was true of the prophet Isaiah (see Isa. 6:6–8) and the same is true today.

In the New Testament, Christians are urged to 'put on the whole armour of God' (Eph. 6:11). This includes having 'your feet [shod] with the preparation of the gospel of peace' (6:15). This is because the Christian message of *peace with God* give us the confidence to stand firm when the devil endeavours to bring about our downfall. It also enables our feet to go far. Our marching orders are clear. We should always be prepared to 'go ... and preach the gospel'; the story of Jesus and His love; the message of peace with God, to people who need to hear it (Mark 16:15; see also Isa. 52:7).

> I hear the words of love,
> I gaze upon the blood,
> I see the mighty sacrifice,
> And I have peace with God.
>
> 'Tis everlasting peace,
> Sure as Jehovah's Name;
> 'Tis stable as His steadfast throne,
> For evermore the same.
>
> The clouds may come and go,
> And storms may sweep my sky—
> This blood-sealed friendship changes not:
> The Cross is ever nigh.
> (Horatius Bonar 1808–89)

The LORD Our Righteousness (Jehovah-Tsidkenu)

'Behold the days are coming,' says the LORD, *'that I will raise to David a Branch of righteousness; a King shall reign and prosper, and execute judgment and righteousness in the earth. In His days Judah will be saved, and Israel will dwell safely; now this is His name by which He will be called:* THE LORD OUR RIGHTEOUSNESS.*'*

(Jer. 23:5–6)

Our text looks forward to the Second Coming of the Lord Jesus Christ. He is great David's greater Son, the King who 'shall reign and prosper, and execute judgment and righteousness in the earth'. However, not only will He *act* righteously when He comes to judge the world (see Acts 17:30–31), but also, He will *be* the righteousness of His people—'this is His name by which He will be called: THE LORD OUR RIGHTEOUSNESS'.

This is what the apostle Paul calls 'the righteousness of God' in his great epistle to the Romans (see Rom. 3:21–26)— not the righteousness of God in punishing sinners, but the righteousness of God in justifying them (i.e. declaring them *righteous* or *not guilty*). Because the Lord Jesus Christ was 'set forth as a propitiation [or sacrifice of atonement] by His blood' (Rom. 3:25a), God can be 'just and the Justifier of the one who has faith in Jesus' (Rom. 3:26b). Justification is more than forgiveness; it is 'just as if I'd never sinned'. The price has been paid! God's justice has been satisfied! The whole world is guilty before God according to the law of Moses but, thank God, those who have faith in Jesus are 'justified from all things' (see Acts 13:38–39). This is 'the righteousness which is from God by faith' (Phil. 3:9).

The Bible presents it to us using accountancy terminology. The classic example is Abraham who 'believed God and it was *accounted to him for righteousness*' (Rom. 4:3). This is well illustrated by the runaway slave Onesimus whom Paul sent back to his master, Philemon, saying, 'if he has wronged you or owes anything, put that on my account ... I will repay ...' (Philem. 18–19). Likewise, our sins were put on the account of the Lord Jesus Christ (see Isa. 53:6). He satisfied justice by dying for them and what He accomplished is put on our account, when we put our trust in Him.

This does not mean that the Lord Jesus Christ became sinful, nor does it mean that we become sinless. Rather it means that the Lord assumed our guilt and bore the punishment for it so that we who trust in Him become 'not guilty' in the sight of God. This is our righteous standing before God and it is all because the sinless Son of God loved us and gave Himself for us. He is indeed 'THE LORD OUR RIGHTEOUSNESS'.

One more thing. We must not overlook the fact that our text says that 'in His days *Judah* will be saved, and *Israel* will dwell safely'. Now, of course, God's wonderful plan of salvation is for the Gentiles as well as the Jewish people. The latter 'stumbled' over their Messiah when He came (see Rom. 9:30–33). However, individual Jews can still be saved by faith in Jesus the same as anyone else (see Rom. 10:11–13), and one day, at or just before the Second Coming, I believe there will be a great turning to

Him among the Jewish people (see Rom. 11:25–26). In that day, many of them will rejoice in Jehovah-Tsidkenu, together with a great multitude of believing Gentiles as well.

> I once was a stranger to grace and to God;
> I knew not my danger and felt not my load;
> Though friends spoke in rapture of Christ on the tree,
> Jehovah-Tsidkenu was nothing to me.
>
> Like tears from the daughters of Zion that roll,
> I wept when the waters went over His soul;
> Yet thought not that my sins had nailed to the tree
> Jehovah-Tsidkenu—'Twas nothing to me.
>
> When free grace awoke me, by light from on high,
> Then legal fears shook me, I trembled to die;
> No refuge, no safety, in self could I see;
> Jehovah-Tsidkenu my Saviour must be.
>
> My terrors all vanished before the sweet name;
> My guilty fears banished, with boldness I came
> To drink at the fountain, life-giving and free:
> Jehovah-Tsidkenu is all things to me.
>
> E'en treading the valley, the shadow of death,
> This watchword shall rally my faltering breath;
> For, when from life's fever my God sets me free,
> Jehovah-Tsidkenu my death-song shall be.
> (Robert Murray M'Cheyne, 1813–43)

The LORD Is There (Jehovah-Shammah)

And the name of the city from that day shall be: THE LORD
IS THERE.

(Ezek. 48:35b)

The city referred to in our text is New Jerusalem. When
the prophet Ezekiel wrote down the last nine chapters of
his book, Jerusalem and its temple were in ruins, but God gave
him a vision of a glorious city and temple, giving great hope for
the future.

I do not think that what Ezekiel saw was fulfilled by the
rebuilding of the earthly city and temple after the seventy years
of exile were ended. The rebuilding we read about in Ezra
and Nehemiah was important, but I think that what Ezekiel
saw was far more glorious than that. It looks forward to the
glorious 'New Jerusalem' that will one day come down from
heaven when the earth is renewed after the Second Coming of
Jesus (see Rev. 21:2).

Some people disagree with this because some of the details
are different. The names of the twelve tribes of Israel are
written on the gates of Ezekiel's city and also on the gates of
the apostle John's 'New Jerusalem' (see Ezek. 48:30–34; Rev.
21:12–13). Also, there is a river of life-giving water flowing
from both cities, with trees on either bank whose 'fruit will
be for food, and their leaves for medicine' (see Ezek. 47:12;
Rev. 22:1-2). However, Ezekiel's city contains a glorious
temple whereas John says concerning New Jerusalem, 'I saw

no temple in it' (Rev. 21:22). Also, John's New Jerusalem is much larger than Ezekiel's glorious city.

Both cities are 'laid out as a square' (Rev. 21:16a), but while the perimeter of Ezekiel's city is 'eighteen thousand cubits' (Ezek. 48:35a) or about 6 miles (based on a long cubit of 21 inches—see Ezek. 43:13), the perimeter of New Jerusalem is forty-eight thousand 'stadia' (Rev. 21:16, NIV) or about 5,600 miles (according to the NIV footnote)! The size of Ezekiel's city was in keeping with the size of Jewish cities in Old Testament times, but the size of John's New Jerusalem is mind-boggling by any standard, especially when one considers that it is twelve thousand stadia high (1,400 miles high) as well! There is certainly plenty of room for all who wish to enter that city one day, just as the Lord Jesus Christ said (see John 14:2–3).

I think the great size of John's New Jerusalem reflects God's purpose to save 'a great multitude' of Gentiles (see Rev. 7:9–10). Yes, the names of the twelve tribes of Israel are written on the gates, but 'the names of the twelve apostles of the Lamb' are written on the foundations (Rev. 21:14). The New Jerusalem is the eternal home of the church as well as Israel.

The other difference between Ezekiel's city and John's is that the latter had 'no temple in it, for the Lord God Almighty and the Lamb are its temple' (Rev. 21:22). In Old Testament times, the temple was the place where God dwelt with His people, especially 'the part ... which is called the Holiest of All' (Heb. 9:3). Only the Jewish high priest was allowed to go into this holiest part 'once a year, not without blood, which he offered for himself and for the people's sins' (Heb. 9:7). However, when the Lord Jesus Christ shed His precious blood on Calvary's Cross, He opened up 'the new and living way' into the presence of God for us (see Hebrews 10:19–20, RSV). This is why, when Jesus 'yielded up His spirit', 'the veil of the temple was torn in two from top to bottom' (Matthew 27:50–51). John's New Jerusalem has no temple in it because God's presence will be manifested throughout the city. 'The Lord God Almighty and the Lamb *are* its temple' (Rev. 21:22). No other temple will be needed.

The glorious temple in Ezekiel's vision assured the people that there was a glorious future ahead in which 'the LORD' (Jehovah) would dwell with His people. This is the meaning of our text, 'THE LORD IS THERE' (Jehovah-Shammah). John's vision does not contradict this, but rather takes it far beyond what the Old Testament people of God could possibly have imagined. That city so bright will shine with 'the glory of God' (Rev. 21:10–11) and 'He will dwell with them, and they shall be His people. God Himself will be with them and be their God' (Rev. 21:3). This is the great thing—not the brightness nor the size nor anything else—our great God and Saviour whom we love will be there:

> And the name of the city from that day shall be: 'THE LORD IS THERE.'

> When by the gift of His infinite grace
> I am accorded in heaven a place,

Just to be there and to look on His face,
Will through the ages be glory for me.

Friends will be there I have loved long ago;
Joy like a river around me will flow;
Yet just a smile from my Saviour, I know,
Will through the ages be glory for me.
(Charles H. Gabriel, 1856–1932)

Part 2: Promises of Jesus

It is a thing most wonderful that 'the Word became flesh and dwelt among us' (John 1:14). The Son of God, the One who is equal with God the Father, became a real man, born of the virgin Mary. He knew what it was to feel hungry, thirsty, tired and in pain. The Bible even says that He 'was in all points tempted as we are, *yet without sin*' (Heb. 4:15). The people, with whom He interacted, beheld a life that was incomparably glorious and heard words spoken with such grace and truth, the like of which had never been heard before—'No man ever spoke like this Man!' (John 7:46).

Such are the promises we are about to consider concerning rest for our souls, Christian fellowship, eternal life and the secret of true satisfaction. There are also two promises concerning the Holy Spirit who was sent forth on the Day of Pentecost into the hearts of all who trust in the Lord Jesus Christ as their Saviour.

The promise
of rest

*Come to Me, all you who ... [are weary and] heavy laden,
and I will give you rest. Take My yoke upon you and learn
from Me, for I am gentle and lowly in heart, and you will find
rest for your souls. For My yoke is easy and My burden is light.*

(Matt. 11:28–30)

These gracious words were spoken by our Lord Jesus
Christ at a time when it was becoming clear that the
Jewish people as a whole were going to reject Him (see Matt.
11:20–24). I have replaced 'labour and are' with 'are weary
and'—either translation is possible (see the NIV).

The promise of rest is in two parts. The first part offers 'rest'
to those who feel their need of it—'all you who are weary and
heavy laden'. Often when we proclaim the gospel, the problem
is that people do not feel their need of it. This is why the law of
the Ten Commandments was given to Israel through Moses at
Mount Sinai. The people said, 'All that the LORD has said we
will do' (Exod. 24:7), but God knew that they would not be
able to. His purpose was to show them that they were sinners
in need of a Saviour.

In his immortal allegory of the Christian life, *The Pilgrim's
Progress*,[1] John Bunyan begins by saying that he 'dreamed a
dream' in which he saw 'a man clothed with rags, standing in
a certain place, with his face from his own house, a book in his
hand, and a great burden upon his back'. The great burden is
explained by Psalm 38:4, where King David says that his sins
were like a heavy burden which was too heavy for him to bear.
Bunyan's Christian set out on his dangerous journey because

41

he too felt the heavy burden of his sins and wanted something done about it.

When people feel this heavy burden, the Lord Jesus Christ steps in and says, 'Come to Me ... and I will give you rest.' This means the rest of conscience that comes from knowing that 'the blood of Jesus Christ [God's] Son cleanses us from all sin' (1 John 1:7). Firstly, the law stirs our consciences—it shows us that we are sinners in need of a Saviour. Then the gospel points us to the remedy, to Jesus the Saviour, 'the Lamb of God who takes away the sin of the world' (John 1:29). The sinless Son of God, equal with God the Father, became Man and went to the Cross for us people and for our salvation. However, there needs to be a response, as our text says. We need to come to the Lord Jesus Christ and put our trust in Him as our own Saviour.

When Bunyan's Christian came to the Cross, 'his burden loosed from off his shoulders, and fell from off his back, and began to tumble, and so continued to do, till it came to the mouth of the sepulchre, where it fell in, and I saw it no more'.[2] The great burden which had troubled Christian in the City of Destruction and weighed him down in the Slough of Despond, which Mr Legality could never have removed from his shoulders, now fell from off his back of its own accord. Burdens are lifted at Calvary and nowhere else. It is only the substitutionary atonement of the Lord Jesus Christ that can remove our guilt and give us rest from the heavy burden of sin.

The second part of the promise speaks about a new 'yoke'. In those days, oxen were yoked together to pull a plough or a cart. The yoke is a symbol of service. The Lord's yoke is not the intolerably heavy 'yoke' of the law which none of us can bear (see Acts 15:10–11), but the 'yoke [which] is easy' of serving the Lord Jesus Christ by love. He is a gentle Master, 'gentle and lowly in heart', and, if we know the joy of salvation through faith in Him, it is no hardship for us to serve Him as our Lord—we love Him and want to do so. I think the 'rest for your souls' promised, goes beyond the rest of conscience we experience when we first trust in the Lord Jesus Christ as our Saviour. It also includes the satisfaction that comes to a loving soul from doing what the Lord wants us to do.

> I heard the voice of Jesus say.
> 'Come unto Me and rest;
> Lay down, thou weary one, lay down
> Thy head upon My breast!'
> I came to Jesus as I was,
> Weary, and worn, and sad;
> I found in Him a resting-place,
> And He has made me glad.
> (Horatius Bonar, 1808–89)

The promise
of fellowship

For where two or three are gathered together in My name, I am there in the midst of them.

(Matt. 18:20)

Christians do not need to be on their own. They can gather together with others in the name of Jesus, which means Saviour (see Matt. 1:21), and when they do, the Saviour Himself promises to be in their midst. Physically, the Lord Jesus is in heaven, seated at the right hand of God the Father, but spiritually, by the Holy Spirit, He is in the midst of His people. This is the promise of fellowship—Christian people gathering together and the Lord Himself in their midst. This is what church is all about.

In Old Testament times, God's dealings with mankind centred upon the nation of Israel, but while He was here on earth, the Lord Jesus Christ said, 'I will build My church' (Matt. 16:18). In the present Christian era, God's dealings with mankind centre upon the church—that worldwide spiritual entity composed of all who genuinely believe and trust in the Lord Jesus Christ as their Saviour. If you believe in Him, you belong to His church and you should gather together with other believers. The Greek word translated 'church' means *an assembly of people* and Christians *should* assemble together to proclaim the gospel, worship God, hear His Word, encourage one another, observe the Lord's Supper and pray.

The Lord's promise to build His church (Matt. 16:18) is the first time the word 'church' is mentioned in the New Testament.

The second occurrence comes two chapters later when the Lord Jesus Christ speaks about discipline in the church—see Matthew 18:15–18. However, the next verse opens up a wider thought by saying that 'if two of you agree on earth concerning anything that they ask, it will be done for them by My Father in heaven' (Matt. 18:19). This needs to be qualified by the fact that our prayers must be according to God's will (see 1 John 5:14), but what an encouragement to corporate prayer! God in heaven will do what we ask, not because we deserve it, but because we are gathered together in the Saviour's name and because the Saviour Himself is in the midst and that to bless us. This brings us to the promise we are considering.

The Old Testament speaks in a similar manner about God being in the midst of His people. For example, Psalm 46:5 says that 'God is in the midst of [Jerusalem] …, she shall not be moved; God shall help her …', and Zephaniah 3:15 says that 'the King of Israel, the LORD, is in your midst; you shall see disaster no more'. In Old Testament times, God was in the midst of Israel and now, in the New Testament era, the Lord Jesus Christ, the second Person of the Trinity, is in the midst of His church.

His presence is not confined to large gatherings. The Lord graciously promises His presence to the twos and threes who gather together. For example, I remember in my late teens regularly attending a prayer group, and I remember with affection the humble, godly Christians who gathered to pray and who graciously tolerated my early attempts at public prayer. It was a small gathering in someone's home, but I can still remember a dear lady referring to our text and joyfully saying, 'We are more than the number!'

Even an informal gathering of two or three Christian friends can, I believe, claim this gracious promise. Next time you have such a gathering, why not pause to have a short time of prayer and seek to enter into the blessedness of fellowship, not only with one another, but also with the Lord Jesus Christ in the midst? Of course, He is with us *always*, even when we are on our own (see Matthew 28:18–20), but there is something special, something extra, when we gather together with others who love the Saviour.

> Jesus, where'er Thy people meet,
> There they behold Thy mercy-seat;
> Where'er they seek Thee Thou art found,
> And every place is hallowed ground.
> (William Cowper, 1731–1800)

The promise
of eternal life

And as Moses lifted up the serpent in the wilderness, even so must the Son of Man be lifted up, that whoever believes in Him should not perish but have eternal life.

(John 3:14–15).

Chapter 3 of John's Gospel records how Nicodemus 'came to Jesus by night, to ask Him the way of salvation and light', as an old hymn puts it. He was impressed by the miracles like many others (John 3:1–2), but he was startled by the reply concerning the need to be 'born again' (John 3:3–4). This is why the Lord Jesus had to explain that it was not a physical rebirth, but a spiritual new birth that was needed (John 3:5–8). As 'the teacher of Israel', Nicodemus should have known about the new birth, but he did not (John 3:9–10).

In the next verses, the Lord Jesus Christ assures Nicodemus concerning the truth of what He was saying and refers to Himself as 'He who came down from heaven ... the Son of Man' (John 3:11–13). This brings us to the promise we are considering. Further explanation was pointless until Nicodemus had experienced the new birth for himself. In our text, the Lord gives Nicodemus an Old Testament analogy and the plain statement that 'even so must the Son of Man be lifted up [to die upon the Cross], that whoever believes [trusts] in Him should not perish but have eternal life' (John 3:14–15). Nicodemus could experience the new birth by trusting in the Lord Jesus Christ as his own Saviour—and so can we!

The Old Testament analogy is a wonderful picture of faith,

looking to God's remedy and receiving immediate salvation. The people of Israel were in the wilderness, on their way from slavery in Egypt to all that was promised to them in Canaan. However, the Bible says that 'the soul of the people became very discouraged on the way. And the people spoke against God and against Moses ...' (Num. 21:4–5). The consequence was that 'the LORD sent fiery serpents among the people, and they bit the people; and many of the people of Israel died' (Num. 21:6). However, in answer to prayer, a remedy was provided. Moses made a bronze serpent, put it on a pole and lifted it up so that everyone could see it. The promise was that *'everyone who is bitten*, when he looks at it, shall live', and so it proved to be (Num. 21:7–9).

The promise to the Israelites dying in the wilderness connects with the 'whoever' of our text. There were and are no exceptions. As soon as the Israelites looked at the uplifted serpent, they received immediate salvation—and so do we, as soon as we look by faith to the uplifted Saviour. The message for the Israelites was 'look and live!', and the message for us is the same—'Even so must the Son of Man be lifted up, that *whoever* believes in Him should not perish but have eternal life.' *This is the promise of eternal life*—'life for a look at the Crucified One', as a well-known hymn puts it.

Finally, note well the word 'must'—'even so *must* the Son of Man be lifted up'. He had to be lifted up, He had to be crucified on that first Good Friday. Immediate salvation is offered freely to us because the Lord Jesus Christ paid the great price of sin upon the Cross. Justice had to be satisfied, the Lord Jesus Christ had to be set forth 'as a propitiation [sacrifice of atonement] by His blood' (Rom. 3:25), so that whoever looks by faith to the uplifted Saviour 'should not perish but have eternal life'.

> There is life for a look at the Crucified One,
> There is life at this moment for thee;
> Then look, sinner, look unto Him and be saved,
> Unto Him who was nailed to the tree.
>
> *Look, look, look and live!*
> *There is life for a look at the Crucified One,*
> *There is life at this moment for thee.*
> (Amelia Matilda Hull, 1825–82)

The promise of
satisfaction

And Jesus said to them, 'I am the bread of life. He who comes to Me shall never hunger, and he who believes in Me shall never thirst.'

(John 6:35)

The *feeding of the five thousand* is one of the best-known of all the mighty miracles performed by our Lord Jesus Christ. However, what happened next is not so well known. The Gospel of John tells us that the next day, the people followed the Lord Jesus Christ to Capernaum. They were hoping that He would give them another free meal, but the Lord said that He had something better to give them. These people did not have much spiritual understanding or desire, but I think it is wonderful how the Lord Jesus met them where they were spiritually (hoping for another free meal) and sought to draw them heavenwards by speaking about 'the food which endures to everlasting life' (see John 6:26–27).

The people spoke about the 'bread from heaven', that was miraculously given to their forefathers at the time of Moses, but the Lord Jesus Christ said emphatically that there was something better on offer, 'the true bread from heaven', of which the manna was only a type and foreshadowing, and He went on to say that this true bread was a Person—'He who comes down from heaven and gives life to the world' (see John 6:31–33).

In reply, the people said, 'Lord, give us this bread always' (John 6:34), but they still only dimly understood what the Lord

Jesus Christ was saying and so He said to them: '*I* am the bread of life. He who comes to *Me* shall never hunger, and he who believes in *Me* shall never thirst' (6:35)—not His teaching, nor His example, but Himself—'Jesus Christ and Him crucified' (1 Corinthians 2:2).

It is good to have a varied diet and it is wonderful that our digestive system can cope with many different types of food. There are some foods that almost everyone eats, like bread and rice. There are other foods that are expensive and only eaten by a few, like caviar and oysters. I am so glad that the Lord Jesus Christ said that He was the Bread of Life. He is not only for a few, but the whole wide world. The Bible says that 'God so loved *the world* that He gave His only begotten Son, that *whoever* believes in Him should not perish but have everlasting life' (John 3:16). Whoever you are, whatever you have done wrong, everlasting spiritual life is offered to you in the Lord Jesus Christ. Have you accepted the offer yet?

The Lord Jesus is the Bread of Life and so is His Word, the Bible. It is the Bible that tells us about Him and it is like food to our souls. If young people want to grow physically, they need food every day. Likewise, if you are a Christian and you want to grow spiritually, read your Bible every day (see 1 Peter 2:2).

Caviar and oysters are not usually considered to be an important part of a standard diet, but bread is, in many cultures. We need it and likewise we need the Lord Jesus Christ, if we are going to have everlasting spiritual life. Moreover, He is all we need. If we come to the Lord Jesus and put our trust in Him, the promise we are considering says that we shall never 'hunger' or 'thirst'. In other words, we shall experience satisfaction in our souls. Some people think that satisfaction is obtained by trying to enjoy what life has to offer or by getting lots of money and possessions, but true satisfaction is found in the Lord Jesus Christ and a Christian never needs to look elsewhere. How the Holy Spirit must be grieved when Christians allow themselves to be allured by the tawdry tinsel toys of this world and lose their appetite for the things of Christ (see Jeremiah 2:13)!

'And Jesus said to them, "I am the bread of life. He who comes to Me shall never hunger, and he who believes in Me shall never thirst"' (John 6:35). *This is the promise of satisfaction.*

> O Christ, in Thee my soul hath found,
> And found in Thee alone,
> The peace, the joy I sought so long,
> The bliss till now unknown.
>
> *Now none but Christ can satisfy,*
> *None other name for me!*
> *There's love and life and lasting joy,*
> *Lord Jesus, found in Thee.*
> (Anonymous)

The promise of
the Holy Spirit

And I will pray the Father, and He will give you another Helper, that He may abide with you forever.

(John 14:16)

Our text is Trinitarian—the three Persons of the Trinity are clearly distinguished. The Person speaking is the Lord Jesus Christ who promises to 'pray the Father', with the assured outcome that 'another Helper' will be given to the disciples. For three years, the Lord Jesus had been their Helper, but now He was going away. Their hearts were filled with sorrow, but the Lord assured them that another Helper would be sent to them. This undoubtedly refers to the coming of the Holy Spirit at Pentecost.

The Holy Spirit is 'the Spirit of truth who proceeds from the Father' (John 15:26). He also proceeds from the Son, in the sense that the Lord Jesus Christ 'prayed the Father' for this great gift and then on the Day of Pentecost sent Him to the disciples. In our text, He is called the 'Helper' or 'Comforter' (KJV) or 'Counsellor' (NIV). The Greek word means *One who is called alongside*, the implication being that He is called alongside in order to help and encourage and guide us.

The Holy Spirit helps Christians in many ways. He is 'the Spirit of truth' who moved men to write the Bible and who now helps us to understand it (see John 16:13); 'the Spirit of grace and supplication' who brings home the gospel to our hearts and helps us to pray (see Zech. 12:10); 'the Spirit of life' who helps us to live a victorious Christian life (see Rom. 8:2);

and 'the Spirit of adoption' who helps us to come confidently and without fear to our Heavenly Father (see Rom. 8:15).

The Holy Spirit is 'the Spirit of God' and 'the Spirit of Christ' (see Rom. 8:9). The Father and the Son are in heaven but, by means of the Holy Spirit, they are present everywhere (see Ps. 139:7–10) and, in particular, they come to dwell in the hearts of those who trust in the Lord Jesus Christ as their Saviour (see John 14:23).

Our text says that the indwelling of the Holy Spirit is a gift. On the Day of Pentecost, the apostle Peter spoke about 'the *gift* of the Holy Spirit' (Acts 2:38). It certainly cannot be purchased with money (see Acts 8:18–20), nor can it be merited by good works; rather the Holy Spirit is received 'by the hearing of faith' (see Gal. 3:2). This is well illustrated by the experience of the Roman centurion Cornelius, his relatives and close friends. They were simply listening to the apostle Peter preaching the gospel with believing hearts, when the Holy Spirit was given to them (see Acts 10:43–44).

The Bible is clear that every true believer in the Lord Jesus Christ has the Holy Spirit and our text promises that He will abide with us forever. The Holy Spirit of God can be grieved by our sinfulness, but He never utterly forsakes those who are trusting in the Lord Jesus Christ as their Saviour. They are 'sealed [by Him] for the day of redemption' (Eph. 4:30). The Holy Spirit abides with us *forever*.

> Our blest Redeemer, ere He breathed
> His tender last farewell,

A Guide, a Comforter, bequeathed
With us to dwell.

He came in tongues of living flame,
To teach, convince, subdue;
All-powerful as the wind He came,
As viewless too.

He came sweet influence to impart,
A gracious willing Guest,
While He can find one humble heart
Wherein to rest.

And His that gentle voice we hear,
Soft as the breath of even,
That checks each fault, that calms each fear,
And speaks of heaven.
(Henriette Auber, 1773–1862)

The promise
of power for
witnessing

But you shall receive power when the Holy Spirit has come upon you; and you shall be witnesses to Me in Jerusalem, and in all Judea and Samaria, and to the end of the earth.

(Acts 1:8)

The Lord Jesus Christ was about to ascend to heaven and a great task lay ahead for His church—a task that is still unfinished—the evangelization of the world. What is the one thing needful for this task, the *'sine qua non'* (Latin for 'without which not') without which we are wasting our time? Is it three years at Bible college or friendship evangelism or seeker-sensitive services? Such things may be good or they may not, but they are not the vital ingredient.

Consider the book of Acts. About 'three thousand souls' were added to the church on the Day of Pentecost as a result of Peter's sermon (see Acts 2:41). What was the secret? Simply this, Peter had received power when the Holy Spirit came upon Him on the Day of Pentecost, as our text says. He was one of 'those who have preached the gospel to you by the Holy Spirit sent from heaven' (1 Peter 1:12). However, this power was not limited to the apostles. 'A great number of people believed and turned to the Lord' when the ordinary Christians, scattered by persecution, 'went to Antioch and began to speak to Greeks also'. Why? Because 'the Lord's hand was with them' (see Acts 8:1–4 and 11:19–21, NIV).

There was a gap of just ten days between the promise of power for witnessing being given and its fulfilment on the

Day of Pentecost. The apostles were told to wait in Jerusalem until the promised power came upon them, but how about ourselves? Should we wait and pray, as they did, until the power comes, or should we just assume that we have the power already and seek to play our part in world evangelization?

The Holy Spirit *has* come and now dwells in the hearts of all who trust in the Lord Jesus Christ as their Saviour (see Gal. 4:6). We no longer need to wait, but we do need to watch and pray. The Holy Spirit of God can be grieved by our sinfulness and the manifestation of His power can be quenched as a consequence (see 1 Thes. 5:19).

Also, we need to find 'the God-dependent life', as Joanie Yoder puts it in her book of that name.[1] God never intended us to live life in our own strength. Weakness is no problem. Rather, it is an opportunity for God's strength to be more fully displayed (see 2 Cor. 12:9a). However, we do need to learn this lesson that nothing worthwhile will be achieved if we attempt to tell others about the Lord in a prayerless, self-confident spirit.

The book of Acts emphasizes the importance of Christians praying together (e.g. Acts 1:13–14; 4:31; 12:5). It is the way we express our dependence upon God. Prayer is very important, whether corporate or individual. Acts 4:31 says:

> And when they had prayed, the place where they were assembled together was shaken, and they were all filled with the Holy Spirit, and they spoke the Word of God with boldness.

Let us pray that, when we speak to others, it will be the same!

There shall be showers of blessing:'
This is the promise of love;
There shall be seasons refreshing,
Sent from the Saviour above.

Showers of blessing,
Showers of blessing we need;
Mercy-drops round us are falling,
But for the showers we plead.
(Daniel W. Whittle, 1840–1901)

Part 3: Promises in the Psalms

The Scofield Reference Bible rightly says that the five books of Psalms 'are revelations of truth, not abstractly, but in the terms of human experience. The truth revealed is wrought into the emotions, desires, and sufferings of the people of God by the circumstances through which they pass.'[1]

The six promises in part 3 reflect this. *The promise of a little that is better than many riches* comes from a psalm which speaks about how the wicked prosper. The next two promises come from Psalms which speak about the troubles through which the people of God have to go. Then there is Psalm 51, written from the anguish of great transgression, Psalm 84, written by a man to whom the worship of God meant everything, and finally, the great Messianic Psalm 110, speaking of the One towards whom all the Old Testament people of God looked forward.

The promise of a little that is better than many riches

A little that a righteous man has is better than the riches of many wicked.

(Ps. 37:16)

A 'righteous man' is someone who is right with God by trusting in the Lord Jesus Christ and Him crucified. What the Saviour accomplished at the Cross is put to their account so that their sins are forgiven and they are declared 'righteous'. (In Old Testament times, this was foreshadowed by the sacrifices of the Tabernacle and the Temple.) Such people show the genuineness of their faith by beginning to do what is right as well. The 'wicked' are the opposite on both counts.

Our text speaks about material possessions and compares 'a little' with 'riches'. It does not consider the case of those who are so poor that they have nothing. In general, the Bible does not encourage this option (e.g. see Prov. 30:7–9). Yes, we are told not to lay up for ourselves treasures on earth, but on the other hand our Heavenly Father knows that we need certain things for this present life and He promises to supply them, so long as we give top priority to the advancement of His Kingdom (see Matt. 6:19, 32–33).

So then, we need a little of this world's goods, but why is it that 'a little that a righteous man has is better than the riches of many wicked?' One reason is because 'the arms of the wicked shall be broken, but the LORD upholds the righteous' (Ps. 37:17)—the wicked will only enjoy their riches for a time, whereas those who are right with God can truly be content because, not only do they have the little of this world's goods that God has given them, but they also have God Himself as their Friend, who has promised to be with them, help them and uphold them (see Heb. 13:5–6).

Another reason for our text is that the riches of the wicked are often ill-gotten. It is a much happier thing to obtain a little honestly. That which you have, though little, is enjoyed much. The early Christians 'ate their food with gladness' (Acts 2:46)—it may have been plain, but they enjoyed it!

So then, 'a little that a righteous man has is better than the riches of many wicked' but would not it be better still if he (or she) had a little more! Not necessarily. The Bible says that 'those who desire to be rich fall into temptation and a snare'. Let us be content with what our Heavenly Father gives us. So many people are discontented, always wanting a little more, but it leads to 'many sorrows' not joy (see 1 Tim. 6:9–10).

Not that there is anything wrong with being rich, as such. It is 'the love of money' that is 'a root of all kinds of evil' (1 Tim. 6:10), not money itself. If God trusts us with riches, we have the privilege of giving generously to support Christian causes. All Christians can know the joy of giving to some extent, out of what their Heavenly Father has given them, but Christians who are well endowed with this world's goods can especially have this joy, if they are 'ready to give, willing to share' (see 1 Tim. 6:17–19).

However, the problem with riches, is that they tend to

make us feel self-sufficient. This was what Agur was afraid of. This was why he prayed, 'give me neither poverty *nor riches*' (Prov. 30:7–9). This was why John Bunyan said, 'Here little, and hereafter bliss, is best from age to age,' in The Pilgrim's Progress.[1]

> I'd rather have Jesus than silver or gold,
> I'd rather be His than have riches untold;
> I'd rather have Jesus than houses or lands,
> I'd rather be led by His nail-pierced hand
>
> *Than to be the king of a vast domain*
> *And be held in sin's dread sway;*
> *I'd rather have Jesus than anything*
> *This world affords today.*
> (Rhea F. Miller, 1894–1966)

The promise of immediate help

God is our refuge and strength, a very present help in trouble.

(Ps. 46:1)

Psalm 46 is known as 'Luther's psalm'. When he and his comrades felt downcast, 'the unflinching Reformer would cheerily say to his friend, Dr Philip Melanchthon, "Come, Philip, let us sing the forty-sixth Psalm"'.[1] Dr Martin Luther's well-known hymn, 'A mighty fortress is our God', is in fact a free adaptation of Psalm 46 and perhaps that is what they used to sing on such occasions.

Our text is the opening verse of the psalm. It assures us that God (in Christ) is a strong safe refuge for sinners. The Bible says that 'God was in Christ reconciling the world to Himself' (see 2 Cor. 5:18–20). Because the Lord Jesus Christ was both God and Man, He was able to become our Kinsman-Redeemer, dying upon Calvary's Cross to pay the price for our sins so that 'whoever believes [takes refuge] in Him should not perish but have everlasting life' (see John 3:16).

However, God is not only our refuge but also our *'strength, a very present help in trouble'*. He promises that He 'will *never* leave [us] … nor forsake [us]' (Hebrews 13:5b), but when Christians are in trouble, He draws especially near. 'Therefore we will not fear', says the psalmist, even though things go badly wrong (see Ps. 46:2–3). There may be a major upheaval in the world around us or major opposition from the forces of evil, but if *God* is our refuge and strength then let us not be afraid. Even though we are having a major struggle with sin within us, let us turn to the God of all grace whose 'helping love no limit knows, our utmost need it soundeth', as another of Luther's hymns puts it ('From deep distress I cry to Thee').

Having described a major upheaval in the natural world, the psalm takes a turn. 'There is a river whose streams shall make glad the city of God,' it says (Ps. 46:4a). This river is the 'river of water of life ... proceeding from the throne of God and of the Lamb' in the new Jerusalem (Rev. 22:1). It symbolizes the everlasting spiritual life that is 'the gift of God ... in Christ Jesus our Lord' (Rom. 6:23b). We cannot see the river as the apostle John did, but even now it flows to all who trust in the Lord Jesus Christ and through them to others, bringing life and strength to our souls (see John 7:37–38).

There is a sort of refrain in Psalm 46. It comes twice, in 46:7 and 46:11, saying, 'The LORD of hosts is with us; the God of Jacob is our refuge.' To say that 'the LORD of hosts is with us,' speaks of overwhelming strength. To say that 'the God of Jacob is our refuge,' speaks of overwhelming grace. The God of Jacob is the God of grace.

Jacob was not 'squeaky-clean'. He resorted to deception and downright lying when he *stole* Isaac's blessing from his older brother Esau. However, Jacob's faith in God was genuine and amazingly, God was not ashamed to be called the God of Jacob. It is *this* God who is our refuge: The God of David—the David who committed adultery and murder; the God of Simon Peter—the Simon Peter who denied his Lord three times with oaths and curses. The God who is our refuge, is the God of grace, the God of sinners—just as Jesus was called 'a friend of … sinners', while here on earth (see Matt. 11:19). Not that sin is unimportant, far from it—it is so important that the Son of God had to shed His precious blood to save us from its consequences—but, as I have said already, God in Christ is a strong, safe refuge for sinners. There is no other.

> A safe stronghold our God is still,
> A trusty shield and weapon;
> He'll help us clear from all the ill
> That hath us now o'ertaken.
> The ancient prince of hell
> Hath risen with purpose fell;
> Strong mail of craft and power
> He weareth in this hour;
> On earth is not his fellow.
>
> With force of arms we nothing can,
> Full soon were we down-ridden;
> But for us fights the proper Man,
> Whom God Himself hath bidden.
> Ask ye, Who is this same?
> Christ Jesus is His name,
> The Lord Sabaoth's Son;
> He, and no other one,
> Shall conquer in the battle.
> (Thomas Carlyle, 1795–1881)

The promise of a deliverance that glorifies God

*Call upon Me in the day of trouble; I will deliver you, and
you shall glorify Me.*

(Psalm 50:15)

In our last meditation, we saw that 'God is our refuge and
strength, a very present help in trouble' (Ps. 46:1). So, when
Christians are in trouble, what should we do? Answer: Call
upon the One who is our refuge and strength and claim His
promise of help and deliverance. This is the import of the
promise before us. It is not a promise for non-Christians. Psalm
50:7–15 is addressed to those who God refers to as 'My people'.
There is no such promise in Psalm 50:16–22, which is spoken
to 'the wicked' (though the implication is that if the warnings
of these verses are heeded, then God will be merciful—He
always hears the cry of the truly repentant). However, those
who are trusting in the Lord Jesus Christ as their Saviour are
encouraged by this great promise of deliverance in v. 15, to call
upon God in their time of need.

King Jehoshaphat was in trouble on the field of battle. He
'cried out' to God then and there and the Bible says that 'the
Lord helped him' (2 Chr. 18:31). Likewise, the apostle Paul
was in so much trouble on one occasion that he says, 'we
were burdened beyond measure, above strength, so that we
despaired even of life'. However, in answer to prayer, God
delivered him (see 2 Cor. 1:8–11).

It can be the same for us. The God of Jehoshaphat and Paul
is our God. Troubles come to teach us that 'we should not trust

in ourselves but in God who raises the dead' (2 Cor. 1:9). Let us trust in this great God, call upon Him, and experience the deliverance which He promises to those who do so. Then, let us give Him the glory, as our text says.

Psalm 107:8 (KJV) says, 'Oh that men would praise the LORD for His goodness, and for His wonderful works to the children of men!' We should speak about what God has done for us and we should say it in such a way that it glorifies Him, not us. Apart from God's goodness and grace, we are good-for-nothing, hell-deserving sinners. The apostle Paul understood this. In fact, he said that *he* was the 'chief' of sinners (1 Tim. 1:15). It is true that on one occasion he said that he 'laboured more abundantly than they all,' but he immediately added, 'yet not I, but the grace of God which was with me' (1 Cor. 15:10).

Sometimes when people are in trouble and experience God's deliverance, they make vows, promising to serve Him. This is not mandatory, but if we do make a vow, then we should be careful to keep it. The verse preceding our text says that we should 'offer to God thanksgiving, *and pay [our]... vows to the Most High*' (Ps. 50:14). Vows are not mandatory, but God *does* want us to promise to serve Him, so long as it is done sincerely and cheerfully. The call to consecration in Romans 12:1 is addressed to those who are already Christians ('brethren') and it is motivated by gratitude ('by the mercies of God'). God wants us to give our lives to serving Him gladly and not because we think we have to (see 2 Cor. 9:7).

I have such a wonderful Saviour,
Who helps me wherever I go;
That I must be telling His goodness,
That everybody should know.

His mercy and love are unbounded,
He makes me with gladness o'erflow;
Oh, He is 'the Chief of ten thousand:'
That everybody should know!

He helps me when trials surround me,
His grace and His goodness to show;
Oh, how can I help but adore Him,
That everybody should know!

My life and my love I will give Him,
And faithfully serve Him below,
Who brought me His wondrous salvation
That everybody should know.

Everybody should know,
Everybody should know;
I have such a wonderful Saviour,
That everybody should know.
Carrie Ellis Breck (1855–1934)

The promise that we shall be whiter than snow

Purge me with hyssop, and I shall be clean; wash me, and I shall be whiter than snow.

(Ps. 51:7)

When we look at the wonderful world that God created, certain colours are prominent. For example, it is lovely to see the blue sky, the green grass and the white snow. I do not think there is anything whiter in the world of nature than a freshly laid carpet of snow.

King David longed to be clean and white like that. He had committed his great sin of adultery with Bathsheba and he felt very dirty before God. However, he believed that God could make him clean again—as white as snow, in fact, whiter! This is the import of the promise we are considering, which is David's prayer.

'Purge me with hyssop, and I shall be clean,' he says. Hyssop was the shrub used to put the blood of the Passover lamb on 'the lintel and the two doorposts' of the Israelite houses when God was about to strike all the firstborn in the land of Egypt (see Exod. 12:21–23). It was also used on other occasions. For example, the epistle to the Hebrews speaks about Moses taking 'the blood of calves and goats, with water, scarlet wool, and hyssop' and using the hyssop to sprinkle the people with blood and also 'the book ... the tabernacle and all the vessels of the ministry'. This is how the people were cleansed and forgiven and this is what David wanted God to do for him (see Heb. 9:19–22).

David wanted to be cleansed from guilt by the atoning blood. He wanted all his dirtiness and defilement to be washed away. 'Wash me, and I shall be whiter than snow,' he prayed. Perhaps he was thinking of the sacrifice of the red heifer mentioned in Numbers 19. The ashes of the heifer were stored and then when someone or something needed cleansing, some of the ashes were put in a container, mixed with water, and then 'a clean person shall take hyssop and dip it in the water' and sprinkle it on whoever or whatever needed cleansing (see Num. 19:17–18). Thus, the washing was with water (which symbolizes the Word of God—see Eph. 5:25–26), but still based upon the atonement provided by the sacrifice of the red heifer.

All of this foreshadows what is ours in the Lord Jesus Christ. His precious blood is the true cleansing agent (see Heb. 9:13–14). When we first put our trust in the Lord Jesus Christ as our Saviour, His precious blood cleanses us once and for all from the guilt of sin and we are 'justified' or declared righteous (Rom. 3:28). When Christians sin, we do not lose our righteous standing before God, but sin still defiles us, hinders our fellowship with God, and robs us of our joy. However, there is a way back to joy and fellowship with God. Because 'the blood of Jesus Christ His Son cleanses us from all sin,' all our dirtiness and defilement can be washed away. The Word of God makes us conscious of sin in the nature and sins in the life. Then, 'if we confess our sins', God can be trusted 'to forgive us our sins and to cleanse us' (see 1 John 1:4–10). How wonderful!

No; not despairingly come I to Thee:
No; not distrustingly bend I the knee.
Sin hath gone over me,
Yet is this still my plea,
Jesus hath died.

Lord, I confess to Thee sadly my sin;
All I am tell I Thee, all I have been.
Purge Thou my sin away,
Wash Thou my soul this day,
Lord, make me clean.

Faithful and just art Thou, forgiving all;
Low at Thy piercèd feet, Saviour, I fall:
Oh, let the cleansing blood,
Blood of the Lamb of God,
Pass o'er my soul!

Then all is peace and light this soul within:
Thus shall I walk with Thee the Loved unseen,
Leaning on Thee, my God,
Guided along the road,
Nothing between.
(Horatius Bonar, 1808–1889)

The promise of grace and glory

The LORD will give grace and glory.

(Ps. 84:11)

Grace is the free, unmerited favour of God. It means that God gives us salvation as a free gift, even though we have not done anything to deserve it. The Bible says, 'For by grace you have been saved ... it is the gift of God, not of works ...' (Eph. 2:8–9).

The word 'grace' appears frequently in our English New Testament, but it also appears, albeit less frequently, in the Old Testament. According to *Strong's Exhaustive Concordance of the Bible*, the Hebrew word translated 'grace' is derived from a word meaning to bend or stoop, the idea being that someone stoops to show kindness to an inferior.[1]

The first mention of the word comes in Genesis chapter 6. Because of the great wickedness of mankind, God purposed to destroy the world with a great flood, '*but*', says the Bible, 'Noah found *grace* in the eyes of the LORD' (Gen. 6:8). The second mention of the word in Genesis is similar—God purposed to destroy the cities of the plain, but He showed '*grace*' to Lot (Gen. 19:19, KJV). In both cases, the grace of God shines forth against a dark background of sin and judgement.

Another example is the city of Nineveh. It was a wicked city like the cities of the plain, and the time for judgement had come—'Jonah cried out and said, "Yet forty days, and Nineveh shall be overthrown!"' (Jonah 3:4). However, the people turned from their evil way and the city was not overthrown.

Why not? Jonah tells us that it was because God is 'a *gracious* and merciful God' (see Jonah 3:10–4:2).

God stooped to show kindness, free unmerited favour, to Noah, Lot and the people of Nineveh. However, the greatest stoop was surely when the Lord Jesus Christ left all the glory of heaven and came down—down to earth, down to Manhood, down to the Cross. He came down and brought grace with Him, grace in all its fullness—marvellous, infinite, matchless grace that is greater than all our sin (see John 1:16–17; Rom. 5:20–21).

We need grace, not only for salvation from judgement, but also for victory in the Christian life and enabling for service. It is the grace of God that makes us what we are (see Rom. 6:14, 12:6–8; 1 Cor. 15:9–10).

We need grace and our text says that God will give it. It says that He will give 'glory' as well. The Bible teaches that 'the LORD will give grace *and glory*' to those who are trusting in the Lord Jesus Christ as their Saviour. 'Glory' is mentioned in Hannah's great prayer after the birth of Samuel. She says, '[The LORD] raises the poor from the dust and lifts the beggar from the ash heap, to set them among princes and make them inherit the throne of *glory*' (1 Sam. 2:8a). Yes, God saves us by His grace from the guttermost 'to the uttermost' (Heb. 7:25). He will give grace *and glory*.

One day, the many dangers, trials and snares of this present life will be over and all those who are trusting in the Lord Jesus Christ will come at last to the place of 'many mansions' (see John 14:2). Then we will praise our Saviour for the *grace* that has lifted us from sin's condemnation and degradation, enabled us to serve and live for Him while here below and then made us 'inherit the throne of *glory*' (1 Samuel 2:8).

Reader, does that include you? If not, I urge you to respond to the gracious invitation of the Bible, which urges you to *come* to Jesus for salvation, just as Noah was urged to '*come* into the ark' and be safe (Gen. 7:1). It is spelt C-O-M-E—'C' stands for children, 'O' stands for old folk, 'M' stands for middle-aged and 'E' stands for everyone. *Everyone* is invited to *come*. Jesus said, 'The one who *comes* to Me I will by no means cast out' (John 6:37).

> Amazing grace! how sweet the sound,
> That saved a wretch like me!
> I once was lost, but now am found;
> Was blind, but now I see.
>
> 'Twas grace that taught my heart to fear
> And grace my fears relieved;
> How precious did that grace appear
> The hour I first believed!
>
> Through many dangers, toils and snares
> I have already come;
> 'Tis grace hath brought me safe thus far
> And grace will lead me home.

When we've been there ten thousand years,
Bright shining as the sun,
We've no less days to sing God's praise
Than when we first begun.
(John Newton, 1725–1807)

The promise of
a willing people

Your people shall be [willing] ... in the day of Your power.

(Ps. 110:3a)

Psalm 110 is undoubtedly a Messianic psalm. It is a psalm of David about his great Descendant, the Lord Jesus Christ, whom David calls, 'my Lord' (Ps. 110:1). David predicts that He will have 'enemies' (Ps. 110:1–2), but also that He will have a *willing* people (110:3a). The NKJV says 'volunteers', but both the KJV and the NIV say 'willing', and I prefer it!

The Bible says that 'whosoever will,' may come (Revelation 22:17, KJV). The Lord Jesus Christ's people are those who willingly and gladly come to Him and put their trust in Him as their Saviour. As the great evangelist D.L. Moody very simply put it, 'the whosoever wills are the elect and the whosoever won'ts, the non-elect!'[1]

We are all *whosoever won'ts* by nature, but our text says, 'Your people shall be [willing] *in the day of Your power*.' It is the power of the Lord Jesus Christ that makes the difference. He sent the Holy Spirit to His disciples on the Day of Pentecost to empower them to proclaim the gospel, so that sinners might be drawn to the Lord Jesus Christ and be willing to trust in Him as their Saviour (see Acts 1:8; John 12:32).

Reader, have you ever felt that drawing power? Are you feeling it now? If so, do not harden your heart, but come and trust in the Saviour *now* (if you have never done so). He is the One who is 'a priest forever according to the order of Melchizedek' (Ps. 110:4). He offered Himself as a sacrifice of atonement at Calvary's Cross, rose again the third day and then sat down 'at [God the Father's] ... right hand' (Ps. 110:1), where 'He always lives to make intercession for [those who trust in Him] ...' (see Heb. 7:24–25). He loves sinners; He died for sinners; He intercedes for sinners! Trust in Him today!

As for his enemies, the Lord Jesus is sitting at God the Father's right hand, waiting until they are made His 'footstool' (Ps. 110:1). This present gospel age is the day of His gracious power by which enemies are turned into friends, but for those who are stubborn (the whosoever won'ts), 'the day of His wrath' is coming when 'He shall judge among the nations' (Ps. 110:5–6a). This will be fulfilled at the Second Coming of Jesus. The Bible says that in that day 'every knee *must* bow' (see Philippians 2:10, AMPC), but this will be a grudging, forced submission on the part of many and will not bring them salvation.

God loves a willing people. He offers salvation 'to every creature' (Mark 16:15), but only the *whosoever wills* accept it and benefit from it. Of course, this is nothing to be proud of. The free gift of salvation is the thing to be proud of, not the fact that we have accepted it (see 2 Cor. 9:15). Moreover, as we have said already, our nature is so perverse and foolish that we never would have accepted the wonderful gift, were it not for the power of the Lord Jesus Christ drawing us to Himself.

What can a willing people do to express their gratitude? They can give their whole lives to God. The Bible's call to consecration is addressed to Christians and it is motivated by gratitude (see Rom. 12:1). God wants us to give our lives to serving Him gladly and not because we think we have to (see 2 Cor. 9:7). However, it is very reasonable because, as the great cricketer and pioneer missionary C.T. Studd put it, 'If Jesus Christ be God, and died for me, then no sacrifice can be too great for me to make for him.'[2]

> O happy day, that fixed my choice
> On Thee, my Saviour and my God!
> Well may this glowing heart rejoice,
> And tell its raptures all abroad.
>
> 'Tis done! The great transaction's done!
> I am my Lord's and He is mine;
> He drew me and I followed on,
> Charmed to confess the voice divine.
> (Philip Doddridge , 1702–51)

Part 4: Promises for the Christian life

In the New Testament, the epistles written by the apostle Paul to the churches invariably begin with a greeting, wishing the Christians to whom he is writing 'grace' and 'peace' (see Rom. 1:7; 1 Cor. 1:3; 2 Cor. 1:2; Gal. 1:3; Eph. 1:2; Phil. 1:2; Col. 1:2; 1 Thes. 1:1; 2 Thes. 1:2). Were he addressing non-Christians, this would probably refer to *saving* grace and peace *with God*. However, these epistles are written to Christians who already have these blessings. Therefore, I believe Paul has in mind the *strengthening* grace and the peace *of God* which we need as Christians, if we are to live victorious Christian lives.

The first three meditations in part 4, consider these blessings of 'grace' and 'peace'. The fourth and final meditation is 'The promise of work to do'. Something is seriously lacking in a Christian life that has an inflow of blessing, but no corresponding outflow of blessing to others. If this is you, do make sure you read the fourth meditation!

The promise
of grace to
the humble

God resists the proud, but gives grace to the humble.

(1 Peter 5:5b)

This is a short but important saying. Anything recorded in the Bible is important, but the promise of grace to the humble occurs three times and so must be very important. The original statement is in Proverbs 3:34. In the New Testament, the Septuagint version (the ancient Greek translation of the Old Testament) of the saying is quoted by the apostle Peter (in our text) and also by James (see James 4:6b). It applies both to salvation and also to the Christian life because we need grace for both.

The Lord Jesus Christ once told a parable about 'two men [who] went up to the temple to pray'. One was a proud man, whereas the other was a humble man. The proud man boasted that he was upright and religious, whereas the humble man could only 'beat his breast, saying, "God be merciful to me a sinner!"' However, the surprise was that it was the self-confessed sinner who went home right with God, not the man who thought he was upright and religious (see Luke 18:10–14). God resists the proud, but gives grace to the humble!

This is why salvation is by grace through faith. It is 'not of works, lest anyone should boast' (Ephesians 2:8–9). If people got to heaven because they had done this or that, they would have something to boast about, but God will not tolerate such pride. When we get to heaven, we will humbly sing words like these:

Unto Him who hath loved us and washed us from sin,
Unto Him be the glory for ever! Amen.

Philip Paul Bliss (1838–76)

The promise to the humble also applies to the Christian life. When Peter wrote down the words of our text, he was writing to Christians. Even though we have learned humility to some extent through the gospel, there is still a lot of pride in us, and God hates pride. I think this is one reason why we go through difficult experiences at times—they make us feel wretched and bewildered, but they teach us greater humility.

For example, King Uzziah was a good and godly king, and 'God made him prosper' (2 Chr. 26:5). The Bible says that 'he was marvellously helped till he became strong. But ...'. Sadly, there is a 'but' in the lives of many true Christians. King Uzziah became proud, intruded into the priestly office, and felt the weight of God's chastening hand as a result (see 2 Chr. 26:15–21). God resists the proud!

Uzziah was brought low until the day of his death, but it does not have to be like that. If we learn to be humbler through the difficult times, God will give us more grace and lift us up again (see James 4:10; 1 Peter 5:6).

John Bunyan sought to show the difficulty Christians have with being humble, in The Pilgrim's Progress.[1] He speaks about Christian having to go down into the Valley of Humiliation and says that 'it is a hard matter for a man to go down into [this valley]'. The Bible says, 'Pride goes before destruction, and a haughty spirit before a fall' (Prov. 16:18), and Christian

learned this by bitter experience when Apollyon 'gave him a
dreadful fall' in the Valley of Humiliation. However, learn it
he did and God raised him up again, and the enemy was put to
flight (see James 4:6–7).

One of the Bible texts on display in my study is this
promise to the humble. It is an important saying. I need to
be reminded of it and perhaps you do too. Let us learn to
be humble. Then we can be sure that 'the God of all grace'
will give us all the grace and help we need, as we go on in
the Christian pathway (see 1 Peter 5:6–11). Let us not be like
proud King Uzziah, but like the humble, contented, child-
like heart set forth as an example to us in Psalm 131 (see Ps.
131:1–3).

> Quiet, Lord, my froward heart;
> Make me teachable and mild,
> Upright, simple, free from art;
> Make me as a little child—
> From distrust and envy free,
> Pleased with all that pleases Thee.
>
> What Thou shalt today provide,
> Let me as a child receive;
> What tomorrow may betide,
> Calmly to Thy wisdom leave:
> 'Tis enough that Thou wilt care—
> Why should I the burden bear?

As a little child relies
On a care beyond his own,
Knows he's neither strong nor wise,
Fears to stir a step alone—
Let me thus with Thee abide,
As my Father, Guard, and Guide!
(John Newton, 1725–1807)

The promise
of grace that
is sufficient

My grace is sufficient for you, for My strength is made perfect in weakness.

(2 Cor. 12:9a)

A great sorrow came into my mother's life when my father was diagnosed as having acute leukaemia. My mother looked after him at home as much as possible. She also prayed that he would get better, but she had no inward assurance that he would. Instead, it seemed as though a promise of Scripture was being spoken to her—the words of our text. This was not what Mum wanted to hear. She missed my father greatly when he died. I was at home at the time, which helped, but it was God's grace that sustained my mother. Dad was the stronger character. People thought that Mum would not be able to cope when he died. But she was. I believe through it all, she had an inner peace and strength that sustained her.

The promise of grace that is sufficient was originally spoken to the apostle Paul. A 'thorn in the flesh' was making life difficult for him and he prayed earnestly 'that it might depart from me'. However, God's answer was the words of our text. When the apostle reflected on this, he was able to say that he took pleasure in life's difficult times. This was because he now understood that when he felt weak, he could rely upon God to make him strong (see 2 Cor. 12:7–10). In Romans 5, he says that Christians should 'glory in tribulations [life's difficult times]', because going through such times leads to a deeper experience and a brighter hope (see Rom. 5:3–4, KJV).

Sometimes Christians pray for a deeper experience and then wonder why things start to get difficult—God is answering their prayers!

Not that God helps us because we deserve it. It is His *grace* that is sufficient for us—His free unmerited favour. Firstly, God saves us from judgement by His grace, just as He saved Noah, Lot and the Ninevites (see 'The promise of grace and glory'). Then He helps us through all the changing scenes of life on the same principle. Moreover, God gives us an abundant supply of His grace—it is *sufficient*, it is all we need, just as it was for the apostle Paul.

God gives us extra strength when we need it. This was Paul's experience. We are not told precisely what Paul's 'thorn in the flesh' was, but it obviously made life difficult for him and he prayed earnestly for its removal, as I have already said. His prayer was answered, but instead of the 'thorn' being removed, Paul was assured that God's grace and strength would be sufficient for him. God would give him extra strength when he needed it, and Paul's weakness was an opportunity for God's strength to be displayed—'My strength is made perfect in weakness,' he was told. God would be glorified in a way that would not be the case if He were simply to remove the 'thorn' (Moreover, the 'thorn' was necessary, for Paul's good, to keep him from pride—see 2 Cor. 12:7).

The same is true for every Christian. See 1 Timothy 1:14–16, where Paul's experience of grace is said to be 'a pattern' that applies to all who trust in the Lord Jesus Christ as their

Saviour. We are not Paul, but the same God who strengthened Paul when he felt weak can strengthen us. Because it is by grace—God's free unmerited favour—none of us are beyond the scope of this.

> The grace of the Lord, like a fathomless sea—
> Sufficient for you, sufficient for me—
> Is tender and patient and boundless and free—
> Sufficient for every need.
> (J. Stuart Holden, D.D., 1874–1934)[1]

The promise of
the peace of God

Be anxious for nothing, but in everything by prayer and supplication, with thanksgiving, let your requests be made known to God; and the peace of God, which surpasses all understanding, will guard your hearts and minds through Christ Jesus.

(Phil. 4:6–7)

In our fourth meditation, The-Lord-Is-Peace (Jehovah-Shalom), I spoke mostly about peace *with* God, but I said, 'There is also the peace *of* God, an inward experience which surpasses all understanding.' This is the promise that we are now considering.

In the Sermon on the Mount, the Lord Jesus Christ told His disciples not to worry about material needs such as food and clothing. However, turning to Paul's epistle to the Philippians, we find that Christians should not worry about anything at all. 'Be anxious for nothing,' says the apostle.

Easier said than done! This present life is full of trouble (see Job 14:1; Acts 14:22). Many things concern us and it is hard not to worry. However, it can be done if we enter into what Paul says next: 'Be anxious for nothing, *but in everything by prayer and supplication, with thanksgiving, let your requests be made known to God.*'

'In everything by prayer and supplication.' There is nothing that we cannot tell our Heavenly Father about. 'What a privilege to carry *everything* to God in prayer,' as the well-known hymn says. Paul says we should come to Him with specific requests, *not forgetting thanksgiving* for the blessings we already have. Our Heavenly Father loves us greatly, and if something concerns us, it is important to Him. We should take our burden to the Lord and leave it there.

If we do this, then we experience the peace of God. God may not answer our prayers immediately, but He does promise 'the peace of God'. It is the peace of knowing that our Heavenly Father knows all about that which concerns us. We place the whole thing trustfully in His hands, knowing that He will do whatever is best for us (see Isa. 26:3).

The peace of God is not outward tranquillity. When Paul wrote his epistle to the Philippians, he was in chains in Rome awaiting possible execution. Nor is the peace of God the same thing as peace with God. The latter is friendship with God, an unchanging relationship (as I said in our fourth meditation), whereas the former is an inward experience which 'surpasses all understanding'. It protects our hearts and minds from the harmful effects of anxiety, and it does this 'through Christ Jesus'—in virtue of who He is and what He has done for us at Calvary's Cross.

What a carefree and happy thing the Christian life ought to be! Not careless, because constant watchfulness is needed, but carefree because we can cast all our care upon the God who loves us so much (see 1 Peter 5:7).

> We bless Thee for Thy peace, O God,
> Deep as the unfathomed sea,
> Which falls like sunshine on the road
> Of those who trust in Thee.

We ask not, Father, for repose
Which comes from outward rest,
If we may have through all life's woes
Thy peace within our breast –

That peace which suffers and is strong,
Trusts where it cannot see,
Deems not the trial way too long,
But leaves the end with Thee;

That peace which flows serene and deep,
A river in the soul,
Whose banks a living verdure keep—
God's sunshine o'er the whole.

O Father, give our hearts this peace,
Whate'er the outward be,
Till all life's discipline shall cease,
And we go home to Thee.
(Anonymous, c. 1858)

The promise
of work to do

For we are His workmanship, created in Christ Jesus for good works, which God prepared beforehand that we should walk in them.

(Eph. 2:10)

Genuine saving faith is a living thing that produces good works as its fruit. The good works do not contribute to our salvation—our salvation is a settled thing before we ever do a single good work that is acceptable to God (see Eph. 2:8–9)—but God still wants us to do them. Our text speaks about those who have been saved by grace through faith. It says, 'For we are His workmanship, created in Christ Jesus *for good works, which God prepared beforehand that we should walk in them.*' This means that God has a plan for our Christian lives. There are things He wants us to do. *This is the promise of work to do.*

The good works that God wants us to do are of two sorts:

- General good works which all Christians should do
- Special good works which vary from Christian to Christian

General good works include things like speaking the truth, giving to those in need, honouring one's parents, and being a good employee or employer—all of these are mentioned later in Ephesians. God is not only interested in special 'Christian' work. The Bible says that whatever job we have (so long as it is honest work), we can do it for God (see Eph. 6:5–8).

However, there are also special good works which vary from Christian to Christian. 'To each his work,' says the Bible

(Mark 13:34). Paul speaks about these special good works in Romans 12:3–8. He starts by saying that we should think about what God wants us to do for Him, guarding against having too high an opinion of ourselves (Rom. 12:3). Then he goes on to say that God's people are 'one body in Christ', but that in a body each member has a different role (Rom. 12:4–5). For example, the mouth does the speaking, the hands do most of the work and the feet take the body to places. Each Christian has a part to play and work to do, and each Christian is given sufficient grace to do what God wants him or her to do (Rom. 12:6a). Seven examples of special good works are given in Rom. 12:6–8, but this list is not exhaustive.

Having something to do is a good thing. Idleness is dangerous. King David should have gone out to battle with his army, but instead he remained at Jerusalem (2 Sam. 11:1). Then he saw Bathsheba and his great sin of adultery with another man's wife followed. Work is good if it is rightly motivated. It keeps us out of mischief and it is also an outlet for blessing to others. God said to Abraham, 'I will bless you … and you shall be a blessing' (Gen. 12:2), and this is true generally. Having received the blessing of salvation, we should work so that others are blessed too.

The Dead Sea is what we would call a *lake*. Water flows into it from the river Jordan, but it has no outlet to the sea proper. The water is so salty that fish and aquatic plants cannot survive in it. It is 'dead'. Some Christians are like the Dead Sea. They lack vitality, and the reason is because they have no outlet for blessing to others.

Those who work for God now will be rewarded when the
Lord Jesus Christ comes again. These rewards are distinct from
salvation. Salvation is by grace whereas rewards are for work
done (see Rev. 22:12). Salvation cannot be lost, whereas rewards
can be—some Christians will miss out on 'a full reward',
whereas others will have the great joy of hearing the Lord say
to them, 'Well done, good and faithful servant' (see 2 John 8;
Matt. 25:21). This is why Christians are urged to 'be steadfast,
immovable, always abounding in the work of the Lord, knowing
that your labour is not in vain in the Lord' (1 Cor. 15:58).

> There's a work for Jesus ready at your hand,
> 'Tis a work the Master just for you has planned.
> Haste to do His bidding, yield Him service true;
> There's a work for Jesus none but you can do.
>
> There's a work for Jesus, humble though it be,
> 'Tis the very service He would ask of thee.
> Go where fields are whitened and the labourers few;
> There's a work for Jesus none but you can do.
>
> There's a work for Jesus, precious souls to bring,
> Tell them of His mercies, tell them of your King.
> Faint not, grow not weary, He will strength renew;
> There's a work for Jesus none but you can do.

Work for Jesus, day by day,
Serve Him ever, falter never, Christ obey.

Yield Him service, loyal, true:
There's a work for Jesus none but you can do.
(Elsie Duncan Yale, 1873–1956)

Part 5: Promises of a reward in heaven

The Bible is crystal-clear that salvation is 'by grace … through faith … not of works lest anyone should boast' (Eph. 2:8–9). However, as I said in our last meditation, Christians who work for God now will be rewarded when the Lord Jesus Christ comes again. Rewards are distinct from salvation. They are something extra.

In the New Testament, the rewards are sometimes referred to as 'crowns.' There are five crowns in all and it seems that they will be awarded for different aspects of faithful Christian service and living. Surely this is where we should place our emphasis as we seek to faithfully serve and live for the Lord in the here and now. The next five meditations consider the promises regarding these 'crowns' one by one.

The promise of an imperishable crown—the serious athlete's crown

Do you not know that those who run in a race all run, but one receives the prize? Run in such a way that you may obtain it. And everyone who competes for the prize is temperate in all things. Now they do it to obtain a perishable crown, but we for an imperishable crown.

(1 Cor. 9:24–25)

Our text speaks about '[competing] for the prize'. This does not refer to salvation. Salvation is a gift to be received not a prize to be won. 'The prize' refers to the 'crowns' which will be awarded for faithful Christian service and living, when Jesus comes again.

Writing to the Christians at Corinth, the apostle Paul calls this prize 'an imperishable crown'. He compares it to the 'perishable crown', the wreath of pine leaves, awarded to the winners of the Isthmian Games. These games were held on the Isthmus of Corinth once every two years and rivalled the ancient Olympic Games in importance. The wreath had little intrinsic value, but it was a badge of honour. Christians who faithfully serve the Lord Jesus Christ will be honoured one day too and the difference is this: the honours of this world are temporary, like the 'perishable crown' of pine leaves, whereas the honours the Lord will bestow are 'imperishable' and eternal.

Athletes are careful about anything that might affect their performance and Paul says that Christians are the same— 'temperate [or self-controlled] in all things'. Paul lived the Christian life like a determined athlete, a serious athlete (see

1 Cor. 9:26–27). He says, 'I discipline my body and bring it into subjection,' and we all need to do this. I trusted in the Lord Jesus Christ as my Saviour as a boy of thirteen and I was filled with joy, but then my body began to assert itself and my Christian life did not really get going until nearly four years later, when God's power broke through into my life afresh at a Christian camp. The apostle Peter warns about 'fleshly lusts which war against the soul' (1 Peter 2:11).

The apostle Paul says, 'I discipline my body and bring it into subjection, *lest, when I have preached to others, I myself should become disqualified*' (1 Cor. 9:27). In saying this, the apostle was not expressing the fear that he could lose his salvation. He knew that absolutely nothing can possibly 'separate [those trusting in the Lord Jesus Christ as their Saviour] … from the love of God which is in Christ Jesus our Lord' (see Rom. 8:35–39). However, he *was* afraid of somehow becoming 'disqualified' and missing out on the prize, the imperishable crown.

We live in a hedonistic day and age and we are well-advised to live a disciplined Christian life, like the apostle. Those 'fleshly lusts which war against the soul' can rob us of our joy and our walk with God now, and they can rob us of the Lord's commendation and reward in a coming day. We need to be careful to confess and forsake our sins, and also to 'lay aside' *anything* that might hinder our progress in the Christian life, even if it is not intrinsically sinful (see Prov. 28:13; Heb. 12:1). *The promise of an imperishable crown is for serious athletes.*

The Lord hath need of me:
His soldier I will be;
He gave Himself my life to win,
And so I mean to follow Him,
And serve Him faithfully.
So, although the fight be fierce and long,
I'll carry on—He makes me strong;
And then one day His face I'll see,
And oh! the joy when He says to me,
'Well done! My brave Crusader!'
(Cecil John Allen, 1886–1973)

The promise of a crown of rejoicing—the soul-winner's crown

For what is our hope, or joy, or crown of rejoicing? Is it not even you in the presence of our Lord Jesus Christ at His coming? For you are our glory and joy.

(1 Thes. 2:19–20)

Our text begins by asking a question: 'For what is our hope, or joy, or crown of rejoicing?' The Christian's hope is the Second Coming of the Lord Jesus Christ. This is what Christians look forward to with great joy. However, there is something extra here—a 'crown of rejoicing'. And what is that? Answer: 'Is it not even you in the presence of our Lord Jesus Christ at His coming?'

The apostle Paul wrote these words to the Christians at Thessalonica. They had been converted when Paul had visited their city and preached the gospel there. The apostle says, 'Our gospel did not come to you in word only, but also in power, and in the Holy Spirit and in much assurance.' As a result, they 'turned to God from idols', and put their trust in the Lord Jesus Christ as their Saviour (see 1 Thes. 1:5,9). It was a great joy to Paul to know that when Jesus comes again, not only would he, Paul, be there in the Lord's presence, but so would these dear people. Their being there on that day would speak for itself. They would be like a badge of honour to Paul, a 'crown of rejoicing'.

However, genuine Christians are not only converts, but also disciples—not only those who say they believe, but also those who prove it by persevering in the Christian way. This is why Paul did not forget about the Thessalonians when he moved on to Athens but sent Timothy back to Thessalonica 'to establish ... and encourage' the new believers (see 1 Thes. 3:1–2). Follow-up is an integral part of gospel work. I think the crown of rejoicing is not only for those who proclaim the gospel to the unsaved, but also for those, like Timothy, who do the follow-up.

I like Proverbs 11:30, which says, 'He who wins souls is wise.' The apostle Paul was a great *soul-winner*. I have to admit that I am not in the same league as him. However, as I look back over the years, I can think of a number of cases where I have either played a part in someone's conversion or else helped with the follow-up. What a joy it is to know that these people are still persevering in the Christian way and what a joy it will be to see them in the Lord's presence one day.

Reader, do you know this joy? When Andrew first met Jesus, he went to his brother Simon 'and said to him, "We have found the Messiah" ... And he brought him to Jesus' (John 1:41–42a). It may not be a brother, but surely there is someone we can pray for and speak to and seek to bring to Jesus. Opportunities can arise in ordinary conversation, if we are on the alert. Also, we can offer people Christian literature or invite them to come with us to a church service or to some special evangelistic event. In addition, we may be able to take part in open-air evangelism or teaching children or young people.

Find another, find another,
Just as Andrew found his brother,
I another soul would bring
To the feet of Christ my King.
(E.H. Swinstead, 1882–1950)

The promise of the crown of righteousness —the Second Adventist's crown

I have fought the good fight, I have finished the race, I have kept the faith. Finally, there is laid up for me the crown of righteousness, which the Lord, the righteous Judge, will give to me on that Day, and not to me only but also to all who have loved His appearing.

(2 Tim. 4:7–8)

Our text comes from the apostle Paul's second epistle to Timothy, his 'fellow labourer in the gospel of Christ,' whom he had sent to establish and encourage the Thessalonians some years before (see 1 Thes. 3:1–2). Timothy was still doing gospel work and Paul sought to encourage him. Then, near the end of his epistle, Paul speaks about himself, saying that his own ministry was almost over (see 2 Tim. 4:6–8).

In our 23rd meditation, we saw that Paul had written to the Corinthians saying that he was like a serious athlete, determined to avoid being disqualified in the race, which is the Christian life. However, now, the race was almost over—he was in the finishing straight, and the crown was in sight. Paul calls it 'the crown of righteousness, which the Lord, the righteous Judge, will give to me', but this raises a question. How can it be righteous to give such a crown to a sinner? Certainly, Paul was an outstanding Christian, but he was still a sinner. In fact, he once referred to himself as the chief of sinners (see 1 Tim. 1:15)!

The answer is, of course, that Paul's sins were atoned for— and so are ours, if we are trusting in the Lord Jesus Christ as our Saviour. Justice was fully satisfied at Calvary's Cross and now it is right and proper for the Lord to notice the good works of His people and reward them. The day of days when Jesus comes again will not only be the solemn day when the unsaved are banished to hell forever. It will also be a day of prize-giving, when 'the crown of righteousness' will be awarded, not only to the apostle Paul, but also to all who can say, as he did, 'I have fought the good fight, I have finished the race, I have kept the faith.'

What was Paul's secret? What keeps a Christian going through all the changing scenes of life? It is love. The apostle says that the prize will be given to 'all who have *loved* His appearing'. If we truly love the Lord Jesus Christ, we will long for His Second Coming and we will be motivated to endure until that wonderful day. This is why I call the crown of righteousness, 'The Second Adventist's crown'.

However, even if we sincerely love the Lord and His appearing, we need to remember that 'the spirit indeed is willing, but the flesh is weak' (Matt. 26:41). The Christian life is a fight to be fought, an ongoing battle with the world, the flesh and the devil. In a short letter to the members of the Radio Bible Class, Revd Richard De Haan once wrote that 'one of the greatest tragedies in the life of a Christian is to come to the end of a fruitful walk with the Lord, only to stumble and fall spiritually. Instead of finishing well, his final days are marked by failures, disappointments, and regrets.'[1] Reader, let us take heed that this does not happen to us. Let us be like Paul, who loved the Lord's appearing and finished well. Let us not be like Demas who 'loved this present world' and forsook

Paul in his hour of need (see 2 Tim. 4:9–10a). He was once Paul's 'fellow labourer' (see Philemon 23–24) and in spite of his failure, perhaps he was a genuine Christian who limped home to heaven in the end, but he was too much influenced by 'this present world'.

> Christian, seek not yet repose;
> Cast thy dreams of ease away;
> Thou art in the midst of foes:
> Watch and pray.
>
> Principalities and powers,
> Mustering their unseen array,
> Wait for thine unguarded hours:
> Watch and pray.
>
> Gird thy heavenly armour on,
> Wear it ever, night and day;
> Ambushed lies the evil one:
> Watch and pray.
>
> Hear the victors who o'ercame;
> Still they mark each warrior's way;
> All with one sweet voice exclaim:
> 'Watch and pray'.
>
> Hear, above all, hear thy Lord,
> Him thou lovest to obey;

Hide within thy heart His word:
Watch and pray.

Watch, as if on that alone
Hung the issue of the day;
Pray, that help may be sent down:
Watch and pray.
(Charlotte Elliott, 1789–1871)

The promise of the crown of glory—the shepherd's crown

And when the Chief Shepherd appears, you will receive the crown of glory that does not fade away.

(1 Peter 5:4)

According to Philippians 1:1, local churches are made up of 'saints', 'bishops' and 'deacons.' 'Saints' is just a way of referring to the people of God in general; 'bishops' means the church leaders—whatever name they may be given; and 'deacons' are those who have a recognised supporting role.

In our text, the apostle Peter is speaking to the church leaders. In the preceding verses, he refers to them as 'elders', 'overseers' and those who 'shepherd the flock of God' (see 1 Peter 5:1–4). The promise of 'the crown of glory that does not fade away,' is for faithful church leaders and Peter tells us what such church leaders look like. You may think this does not apply to you if you are not a church leader, but I believe it is important for all Christians to understand what faithful church leaders look like.

I think there is a shortage of such men in the United Kingdom (I believe 1 Tim. 2:12 precludes women from being church leaders). Back in September 2012, an article appeared in *The Evangelical Times*, entitled 'Where are the ministers?'[1] It said that 'many evangelical churches that can afford to support and are actively looking for a minister are unable to find one.' The article went on to say that we need to pray that 'the Lord of the harvest [would] raise up a new generation of suitable men,' and also that we should value the existing church leaders that we do have and treat them with due respect.

Of course, no church leader is infallible. Even the apostle Peter got it badly wrong on one occasion and had to be 'withstood', because it was a serious matter (see Gal. 2:11–21). However, in general, we should seek to encourage faithful church leaders and avoid giving them a hard time.

So then, what do faithful church leaders look like? Peter gives us a good description in a few words. Firstly, they are those who 'shepherd' or 'feed' the people of God (1 Peter 5:2a). This was what the Lord Jesus Christ told Peter to do when he was recommissioned. The apostles were called to be shepherds as well as fishers and this applies to all who preach God's Word (see Matt. 4:18–19; John 21:15–17). 'Catching' people is only the start—Christians need to be 'fed' with the Word of God so that they can grow spiritually (see 1 Peter 2:2). This is why church leaders must be 'able to teach' the Word of God to others (see 1 Tim. 3:2).

Secondly, faithful church leaders are those who really care about the people of God. They do the job 'not by compulsion but willingly'. They do not need the lure of a high salary—they '[serve] as overseers … not for dishonest gain but eagerly' (see 1 Pet. 5:2b).

Thirdly, faithful church leaders do not lord it over those entrusted to them (see 1 Peter 5:3a). I think this is a danger for otherwise faithful church leaders. It may be easier to pull rank to get one's own way, but the wishes of the congregation as a whole should be treated with due respect.

Fourthly and finally, faithful church leaders practise what they preach. They are 'examples to the flock' (see 1 Peter 5:3b). This is vital:

> Practise what you preach,
> Do the things you teach,
> Then you'll surely reach
> The others all around.
> A.F. Mordaunt Smith
> (Dates unknown)[2]

Church leaders who look like this are of great worth and, when the Chief Shepherd appears, He will show how much He values them by giving them 'the crown of glory that does not fade away'.

The promise of the crown of life—the sufferer's crown

Do not fear any of those things which you are about to suffer. Indeed, the devil is about to throw some of you into prison, that you may be tested, and you will have tribulation ten days. Be faithful until death, and I will give you the crown of life.

(Rev. 2:10)

These words were spoken by the Lord Jesus Christ Himself to the church in Smyrna. A time of fierce persecution and suffering lay ahead of them. When such is the lot of God's people, it is the devil who is behind it—whoever the human agents may be. However, it is God who is on the throne—not the devil. Suffering can only happen if God permits it to happen for some good purpose and it can only last as long as He permits it to last. In this case, God's good purpose was obviously so that the testing time would show them to be genuine faithful Christians.

As regards the time limit on the suffering, some Bible commentators say that the suffering of the local church in Smyrna was a foreshadowing of what would happen to the worldwide church and that the 'ten days' refer to ten periods of fierce persecution. For example, Dr Harry Ironside says, 'It is significant that in the two centuries of Roman persecution which began with Nero and which terminated AD 312, there were ten distinct edicts demanding that governors seek out Christians everywhere and put them to death. The last was under Diocletian. He was the tenth persecutor. The early Christians believed he would be the last, and he was.'[1]

Pagan Rome became holy Rome and for a time fierce persecution ceased. However, as time went by, the Roman Catholic church itself became a persecutor. It dominated Western Europe in the Middle Ages and persecuted true believers in the Lord Jesus Christ just as fiercely as paganism had done previously. Many were burnt at the stake, including the Protestant bishops, Hugh Latimer and Nicholas Ridley, who were martyred during the reign of the Roman Catholic Queen, Mary in 1555. It was Hugh Latimer who famously said, 'Be of good comfort Master Ridley, and play the man. We shall this day light such a candle by God's grace in England as I trust shall never be put out!'[2]

Since the Toleration Act in 1689, Bible-believing evangelical Christians in the United Kingdom have not in general been fiercely persecuted. However, the times they are a-changin', as the well-known song says. I think that British Christians need to wake up to the possibility that a time of fierce persecution and suffering is ahead. Of course, in many parts of the world such suffering is a grim present reality. This is scary, but the Lord Jesus Christ is on the throne and He tells us to not be afraid. Let us put our trust in Him and seek to be faithful, come what may. To those who are faithful to the end, in the midst of suffering, whether they die as martyrs or not, the Lord promises the crown of life. Of course, all Christians are given everlasting life as soon as they put their trust in the Lord Jesus Christ as their Saviour (John 5:24), but this is something extra—the reward for ongoing faithfulness through a time of suffering.

I do not think we need to limit this to suffering as a result of persecution. Just as whatever we do can be done 'as to the Lord'—whether secular employment or playing a musical instrument or whatever (see Colossians 3:23)—even so, whatever we suffer can be suffered for His sake. For example, think of Christians confined because of illness or infirmity for years. What a trial! And how wonderful when there is no complaint, but ongoing faithfulness in seeking to turn this wretched condition into something that is for the Lord's glory.

Finally, James says that the crown of life will be awarded to those who endure temptation (see James 1:12). This fits in with it being 'the sufferer's crown', because being tempted is a form of suffering to anyone who genuinely wants to follow God's way, just as it was for the Lord Himself (see Heb. 2:18, KJV).

> The Son of God goes forth to war,
> A kingly crown to gain;
> His blood-red banner streams afar:
> Who follows in His train?
> Who best can drink His cup of woe,
> Triumphant over pain,
> Who patient bears his cross below,
> He follows in His train.
>
> The martyr first, whose eagle eye
> Could pierce beyond the grave,

Who saw his Master in the sky,
And called on Him to save:
Like him, with pardon on his tongue
In midst of mortal pain,
He prayed for them that did the wrong:
Who follows in His train?

A glorious band, the chosen few
On whom the Spirit came,
Twelve valiant saints, their hope they knew,
And mocked the cross and flame:
They met the tyrant's brandished steel,
The lion's gory mane;
They bowed their necks the death to feel:
Who follows in their train?

A noble army, men and boys,
The matron and the maid,
Around the Saviour's throne rejoice,
In robes of light arrayed:
They climbed the steep ascent of heaven
Through peril, toil, and pain;
O God, to us may grace be given
To follow in their train.
(Richard Heber, 1783–1826)

Part 6: Promises of a glorious future

There is a glorious future ahead for the Christian. We can be sure about this because of the promises of God. In this final part of *Thirty more sparkling gems*, we consider three such promises.

Firstly, we consider the promise of a great innumerable multitude, drawn from every nation under heaven, standing before the Throne of God, who, with jubilant voices, praise Him for salvation. Secondly, there is the wonderful promise that God is still interested in His ancient people Israel and that one day many of them will put their trust in Jesus. Finally, there is the awesome promise of new heavens and a new earth where everything will be right and as it should be.

The promise of a great multitude

Then He brought him outside and said, 'Look now toward heaven, and count the stars if you are able to number them.' And He said to him, 'So shall your descendants be.'

(Gen. 15:5)

The Jewish nation is still greatly loved by God for the sake of Abraham, Isaac and Jacob (see Rom. 11:28), and it still has a special place in His purposes, as we shall see in our next meditation. However, the spiritual descendants of Abraham are 'all those who believe', as he did, whether Jewish or not (Rom. 4:11–12). Abraham's faith believed the promises of God and looked forward to the coming of the Lord Jesus Christ in whom those promises would be fulfilled (e.g. John 8:56, Heb. 11:13). So, if we believe the promises of God and trust in the Lord Jesus Christ as our Saviour, then we are 'sons of Abraham' (Gal. 3:7).

In Genesis 15, God came to Abraham saying, 'Do not be afraid, Abram: I am your shield, your exceedingly great reward' (Gen. 15:1). This was God's promise, but Abraham was not so sure. He was thinking about another promise that God had made, saying, 'I will make you a great nation' (Gen. 12:2a). He was now getting on in years and he still had no offspring—not even one, let alone a great nation (see Gen. 15:2–3)!

At this point 'the word of the LORD' came to Abraham. Even though it was 'a vision', the emphasis is upon what God said rather than what Abraham saw. God promised that Abraham's own flesh and blood would be his heir, through whom the promise of a great nation would be fulfilled (see Gen. 15:4). This brings us to our text, where God says to Abraham: 'Look now toward heaven, and count the stars if you are able to number them.' Abraham was unable to do this and so are we. Thousands are visible to the naked eye on a clear night and, when viewed through a powerful telescope, many millions are visible. God said to Abraham, 'So shall your descendants be.' *This was the promise of a great multitude*—'as many as the stars of the sky in multitude—innumerable as the sand which is by the seashore' (Heb. 11:12).

The apostle John had a vision of this great multitude. He said:

> After these things I looked, and behold, a great
> multitude which no one could number, of all nations,
> tribes, peoples, and tongues, standing before the throne
> and before the Lamb, clothed with white robes, with
> palm branches in their hands, and crying out with a
> loud voice, saying, 'Salvation belongs to our God who
> sits on the throne, and to the Lamb!' (Rev. 7:9–10).

This great company of people, who are trusting in 'the Lamb', the Lord Jesus Christ, for salvation, will be composed of 'all nations, tribes, peoples, and tongues'. Their robes are white because they 'washed [them] ... and made them white in the blood of the Lamb' (see Rev. 7:13–14), and with palm branches and jubilant voices they praise God for salvation. This is the great multitude promised to Abraham and it is the great unfinished task of the church to go and gather them in (see Mark 16:15)!

We have heard the joyful sound:
Jesus saves!
Spread the tidings all around;
Jesus saves!
Bear the news to every land,
Climb the steeps and cross the waves;
Onward! 'tis our Lord's command:
Jesus saves!

Sing above the battle's strife:
Jesus saves!
By His death and endless life,
Jesus saves!
Sing it softly through the gloom,
When the heart for mercy craves;
Sing in triumph o'er the tomb:
Jesus saves!

Give the winds a mighty voice:
Jesus saves!
Let the nations now rejoice:
Jesus saves!
Shout salvation full and free,
Highest hills and deepest caves;
This our song of victory:
Jesus saves!
(Priscilla Jane Owens, 1829–1907)

The promise
that all Israel
will be saved

For I do not desire, brethren, that you should be ignorant of this mystery, lest you should be wise in your own opinion, that blindness in part has happened to Israel until the fullness of the Gentiles has come in. And so all Israel will be saved, as it is written: 'The Deliverer will come out of Zion, and He will turn away ungodliness from Jacob.'

(Rom. 11:25–26)

In Old Testament times, God's dealings with mankind centred upon the nation of Israel, but in the present Christian era, God's dealings with mankind centre upon the church. Does this mean that God is not interested in Israel anymore? This is the question the apostle Paul asks in his great epistle to the Romans (see Rom. 11:1). He himself was a Jew who had responded to the gospel and he was not the only one. He refers to Elijah, who, in a time of depression, thought he was the only true believer left in Israel, but was assured that there were 'seven thousand men who have not bowed the knee to Baal' (Rom. 11:2–4). Even now, says Paul, in the present Christian era, 'there is a remnant according to the election of grace' (Rom. 11:5–6), and one day, as our text says, '*all* Israel will be saved'.

The present situation is that the majority of Jewish people have stumbled and been blinded (Rom. 11:7–10), but this is not intended to be permanent. 'Certainly not!' says Paul (Rom. 11:11a). Yes, 'salvation has come to the Gentiles', but this is 'to provoke [the Jewish people] ... to jealousy', that is, to cause them to want this wonderful salvation as well (Rom. 11:11b).

In the next four verses, Paul anticipates a time when the Jewish people as a whole will know 'fullness' and 'acceptance' (11:12–15). The present situation is described as 'their fall', 'their failure' and their being cast away', and this has led to wonderful consequences—'riches for the world', 'riches for the Gentiles' and 'the reconciling of the world'. In other words, because the Jewish people rejected their Messiah, the gospel of a crucified and risen Saviour is going throughout the world, bringing untold blessing (It was essential to God's plan of salvation that Jesus *should be* rejected and crucified at His first coming—see Acts 2:23). 'Now', says Paul, 'how much more' will the blessing be, if many Jewish people believe in Jesus.

This does not mean that the Old Testament Jewish primacy within the people of God will be reinstated. Paul explains what he means by comparing Israel to an olive tree. Some of the branches have been broken off because of unbelief, so that the Gentiles can be grafted in, but once God's purpose for the Gentiles is complete, the Jewish people as a whole will be grafted in again, if they put their trust in Jesus (Rom. 11:16–24). The highly regarded commentary on Romans by Robert Haldane helpfully speaks about the possibility, probability and certainty of the future conversion and acceptance of Israel.[1] The *possibility* is mentioned in 11:23—'They also, if they do not continue in unbelief, will be grafted in, for God is able to graft them in again.' The *probability* is mentioned in 11:24—the argument here is that the grafting in of 'natural branches' is easier than the grafting in of branches from the wild Gentile olive tree.

The *certainty* of the future conversion and acceptance of Israel is stated in our text. Paul says, 'Blindness in part has happened to Israel', but this is only 'until the fullness of the Gentiles has come in' (Rom. 11:25). As we saw in our last meditation, God's wonderful purpose for the present age is that a great multitude should be saved from all nations and should be included in His people. Once they have 'come in', the blindness will be taken away from Israel 'and so *all* Israel will be saved' (Romans 11:26a), and not just a small remnant, as at present. I think this means that shortly before the Lord Jesus Christ comes again, there will be a great turning to Him among the Jewish people who are alive and remain at that time. Many will put their trust in Him and be saved—this is the 'fullness' spoken of in 11:12. This is supported by the quotation from Isaiah 59:20 in our text—when Jesus comes again, He 'will turn away ungodliness from Jacob' (Romans 11:26b).

> Great God of Abraham! hear our prayer;
> Let Abraham's seed Thy mercy share:
> O may they now at length return
> And look on Him they pierced, and mourn!
>
> Remember Jacob's flock of old;
> Bring home Thy wanderers to Thy fold;
> Remember too Thy promised word,
> 'Israel at last shall seek the Lord.'

Though outcasts still, estranged from Thee,
Cut off from their own olive-tree,
Why should they longer such remain?
For Thou canst graft them in again.

Lord, put Thy law within their hearts,
And write it in their inward parts;
The veil of darkness rend in two,
Which hides Messiah from their view.

O haste the day, foretold so long,
When Jew and Greek, a glorious throng,
One house shall seek, one prayer shall pour,
And one Redeemer shall adore!
(Thomas Cotterill, 1779–1823)

The promise of new heavens and a new earth

But the day of the Lord will come as a thief in the night, in which the heavens will pass away with a great noise, and the elements will melt with fervent heat; both the earth and the works that are in it will be burned up ... Nevertheless we, according to His promise, look for new heavens and a new earth in which righteousness dwells.

(2 Peter 3:10, 13)

In my book, *Thirty Sparkling Gems*, I said, 'What a truly awesome event the Second Coming will be. The whole universe will be shaken by it.' This is true, but the apostle Peter goes further. Our text says that the whole universe will be 'burned up' and replaced by 'new heavens and a new earth'! This promise of new heavens and a new earth was originally revealed to the prophet Isaiah and it is a glorious prospect (see Isa. 65:17–25).

The created heavens are what we usually refer to as the atmosphere and outer space. It is these, together with the earth, which will be 'burned up'. 'The third heaven' will be unaffected. This is the abode of God which has always existed and was not created. In 2 Corinthians 12:2–4, the apostle Paul speaks about being 'caught up to the third heaven,' meaning that he was caught up into the very presence of God.

As regards the created heavens and the earth, I think there will be a connection between the old and the new. The old were created out of nothing, but I think that when they are burned up, God will take the ashes and rebuild them into the new. The epistle to the Romans says that 'the whole creation groans and labours with birth pangs together until now' (Rom. 8:22)—'birth pangs' not 'death throes'! The creation has a future, even though it must be burned up and rebuilt.

Jerusalem, the metropolis of God's people, also has a future. The new Jerusalem is the wonderful place that God has prepared for His people (see John 14:2–3; Heb. 11:16). At present, it is located 'above' in the third heaven (Gal. 4:26), but when the created heavens and the earth have been rebuilt, it will come down to the new earth, and so will God Himself, to dwell with His people (see Rev. 21:1–3).

What will the renewed universe be like? Peter's answer is very brief—he says that it will be a world 'in which righteousness dwells'. Those who dwell there will be right with God and they will do right to other people. Nothing will be wrong and nothing will go wrong. There will be no more hurricanes and earthquakes. Man's inhumanity to man will be no more, and so will man's alienation from God. God says in His Word, 'It shall come to pass that before they call, I will answer; and while they are still speaking, I will hear. The wolf and the lamb shall feed together, the lion shall eat straw like the ox, and dust shall be the serpent's food. They shall not hurt nor destroy in all My [renewed universe] ...' (Isa. 65:24–25).

Finally, I think we should take some notice of Peter's question in 2 Peter 3:11–12:

> Therefore, since all these things will be dissolved, what
> manner of persons ought you to be in holy conduct

and godliness, looking for and hastening the coming of the day of God, because of which the heavens will be dissolved, being on fire, and the elements will melt with fervent heat?

Surely, we should be very different in conduct from the sinful world around us, having reverence for God and His Word—in keeping with the glorious new world that is coming. Let us look forward to that and do what we can to hasten its coming. The reason why the Second Coming of Jesus is delayed is because God is giving people the opportunity to repent and be saved (see 2 Peter 3:9). However, once the gospel has been 'preached in all the world as a witness to all the nations', and once 'the fullness of the Gentiles has come in', '*then* the end will come' (see Matt. 24:14; Rom. 11:25–26).

> Our Lord is now rejected and by the world disowned,
> By the many still neglected and by the few enthroned;
> But soon He'll come in glory! The hour is drawing nigh,
> For the crowning day is coming by-and-by.
>
> The heavens shall glow with splendour; but brighter
>   far than they,
> The saints shall shine in glory, as Christ shall them array:
> The beauty of the Saviour shall dazzle every eye,
> In the crowning day that's coming by-and-by.
>
> Our pain shall then be over, we'll sin and sigh no more,
> Behind us all of sorrow and naught but joy before:

A joy in our Redeemer, as we to Him are nigh,
In the crowning day that's coming by-and-by.

Let all that look for hasten the coming joyful day,
By earnest consecration, to walk the narrow way:
By gathering in the lost ones, for whom our Lord did die,
For the crowning day that's coming by-and-by.

Oh, the crowning day is coming! Is coming by-and-by!
When our Lord shall come in power and glory from
  on high!
Oh, the glorious sight will gladden each waiting
  watchful eye,
In the crowning day that's coming by-and-by.

Endnotes

Part 1: What God Promises To Be To His People

1 John J. Davis, *Moses and the gods of Egypt* (Grand Rapids, MI: Baker Book House, 1991), pp. 72–73.

1. The-Lord-Will-Provide (Jehovah-Jireh

1 Prof. Roland Bainton, *Here I stand: A life of Martin Luther* (Peabody, MA: Hendrickson Publishing Group, 2012), p. 384.

2. The Lord Who Heals You (Jehovah-Rapha)

1 *Strong's Exhaustive Concordance of the Bible: Hebrew and Aramaic Dictionary,* Reference no 7495 (Edinburgh: Thomas Nelson Publishers, 1995), p. 134.

4. The-Lord-Is-Peace (Jehovah-Shalom)

1 *The New Compact Bible Dictionary* (Grand Rapids, MI: Zondervan Publishing Company, 1967), p. 33.

7. The promise of rest

1 John Bunyan, *The Pilgrim's Progress* (Edinburgh: Banner of Truth, 1990), p. 1.

2 Bunyan, *The Pilgrim's Progress*, pp. 35–36.

12. The promise of power for witnessing

1 Joanie Yoder, *Finding the God-dependent Life* (Grand Rapids, MI: Discovery House, 1992).

Part 3: Promises in the Psalms

1 *The Scofield Reference Bible: 1917 Edition*, (Oxford University Press), p. 599.

13. The promise of a little that is better than many riches

1 John Bunyan, *The Pilgrim's Progress*, p. 282.

14. The promise of immediate help

1 C.H. Spurgeon, *The Treasury of David: Volume 1* (Peabody, MA: Hendrickson Publishing Group, 1988), p. 344

17. The promise of grace and glory

1 Strong's *Exhaustive Concordance of the Bible: Hebrew and Aramaic Dictionary,* Reference no 2580, p. 45.

18. The promise of a willing people

1 Dr H.A. Ironside, *Addresses on the Gospel of John* (New Jersey: Loizeaux Brothers, 1980), p. 252.

2 Tiimothy Alford, 'C.T. Studd (1860–1931)', *Evangelical Times*, Nov 2010, p. 27.

19. The promise of grace to the humble

1 John Bunyan, *The Pilgrim's Progress*, p. 58.

20. The promise of grace that is sufficient

1 J. Stuart Holden, D.D. (1874–1934), 'The grace of God'. *Scripture Union Choruses* (Scripture Union, 1964), no. 273.

24. The promise of a crown of rejoicing—the soul-winner's crown

1 E.H. Swinstead (1882–1950), 'Find another, find another', *Scripture Union Choruses* (Scripture Union, 1964), no. 367.

25. The promise of the crown of righteousness—the Second Adventist's crown

1 Revd Richard De Haan, Personal hand-written card.

26. The promise of the crown of glory—the shepherd's crown

1 Bill Dyer, 'Where are the ministers?', *Evangelical Times*, 01 September 2012. https://www.evangelical-times.org/where-are-the-ministers/. Sourced 03 June 2022.

2 A.F. Mordaunt Smith (Dates unknown), 'Practise what you preach', *Scripture Union Choruses* (Scripture Union, 1964), no. 433.

27. The promise of the crown of life—the sufferer's crown

1 Dr H.A. Ironside, *Lectures on the Book of Revelation* (New Jersey: Loizeaux Brothers, 1982), p. 41.

2 Hugh Latimer, cited in: Sir Marcus Loane, *Masters of the English Reformation* (Edinburgh: Banner of Truth, 2005), p. 165.

29. The promise that all Israel will be saved

1 Robert Haldane, *Commentary on Romans* (Grand Rapids, MI: Kregel Publishers, 1996), p. 548.